The Krankies

FAN DABI DOZI

Our Amazing True Story

The Krankies

FAN DABI DOZI

Our Amazing True Story

By Ian and Janette Tough
The Krankies

JOHN BLAKE

Published by John Blake Publishing Ltd,
3, Bramber Court, 2 Bramber Road,
London W14 9PB, England

www.blake.co.uk

First published in hardback in 2004

ISBN 1 84454 026 X

British Library Cataloguing-in-Publication Data:

A catalogue record for this book is available from the British Library.

Design by www.envydesign.co.uk

Printed in Great Britain by CPD, Wales

1 3 5 7 9 10 8 6 4 2

Papers used by John Blake Publishing are natural,
recyclable products made from wood grown in sustainable forests.
The manufacturing processes conform to the environmental
regulations of the country of origin.

Every attempt has been made to contact the relevant copyright-holders,
but some were unobtainable. We would be grateful if the appropriate
people could contact us.

CONTENTS

	Foreword	vii
	Introduction	ix
1	The Toughs Get Going	1
2	Putting on an Act	17
3	The Krankies ... 'Til Death Us Do Part	41
4	The Big Time for Wee Jimmy	47
5	The Yankees Meet The Krankies	61
6	TV on the CV	69
7	Sun, Sea ... and Success	81
8	What a Dope!	105
9	Cracking Television	119
10	Ding Dong	131
11	The Egos Have Landed	151
12	Join the Klub	163
13	It's Wizard in Oz	179
14	Air Today ... Gone Tomorrow	191
15	Look Who's Stalking	205
16	Up for the Craic with Dawn	219
17	Let Me Entertain You	231
18	Absolutely Fan-Dabulous	241
	Epilogue	253

FOREWORD

The Krankies were reared in variety theatres and their know-how and experience is a bonus for any promoter. Should the promoter need a ten-minute spot from an act, they will provide. If he needs a front cloth of two minutes, they can do it. Should they be needed to work through a full two hours, then the Krankies' experience shines through.

I have known Janette since she was a small girl (was she ever any bigger?) and she has used that pocket-size personality to have audiences rocking with laughter at her antics. Ian is the feed (Straight Man) and sets up Janette's approach to raising the laughs, which she never fails to do with her perfect timing and great use of her knowledge of comedy.

They come via the hard school of variety artists. They have a large young following but never needed to deviate from the family humour that audiences trust, and though cheeky they never worried parents with any doubtful material.

Off stage they are quite simply the nicest people you could meet; Ian is an incredible chef and can muster up a banquet at short notice – a banquet, I might add, that makes him chef supreme for an evening at home. My wife Blossom and I have attended many of these gourmet evenings in Australia and enjoyed several hours laughing at their spontaneity and memories of early days in Glasgow's theatres where, if the audiences like you, they'll love you for ever – but if you fall flat they'll remain unenthusiastic to say the very least.

I don't like to call past performers 'Old Timers', instead I prefer to call them survivors, and may the good lord look after The Krankies because they are survivors that need looking after. May he smile on them the way audiences at home and abroad do 'the noo'.

They are rare, talented and among my favourite people on earth.

Sincerely

Max Bygraves, 2004

INTRODUCTION

Husband-and-wife team Ian and Janette Tough became one of Britain's best-loved comedy duos as The Krankies, rocketing to fame at *The Royal Variety Performance* when they delighted the Queen Mum and a television audience of millions in 1978.

Almost 11 years on, national prime-time TV was to follow as they went on to present – and revive – the flagging BBC1 institution *Crackerjack*, captivating and infuriating a nation in equal measures with their catchphrase 'Fan Dabi Dozi'.

Like Morecombe and Wise before them, they were then poached by the BBC's rivals ITV, to headline their Saturday evening line-up.

After three seasons, the BBC decided they needed The Krankies back, and so in 1987 made them an offer they couldn't refuse.

But times were changing and, by the early 1990s, Political Correctness was the phrase buzzing around the corridors of power in TV world.

Suddenly, after nearly a quarter of a century in showbiz, The Krankies were deemed 'seedy', as newly elected panels of 'morality police', employed by the television companies, believed there was something suspect about a husband-and-wife act in which the woman dressed up as a cheeky schoolboy.

The Krankies were now social pariahs and no TV producer wanted to know them. They had had it rough before but, after so much success, this time it was even harder to take.

They had become the butt of showbiz jokes, a punchline for the new breed of brutal TV presenters and the shock jocks who now cluttered the airwaves.

But they dusted themselves down and continued to do panto, started working the cruise-ship circuits, toured Australia during our harsh winter months every year and played a lot of golf.

By the end of the 1990s, after nearly ten years away from TV, their fortunes began to change for the better as they earned the coveted 'cult status' thanks to hilarious appearances on hit comedy shows, including *French and Saunders* (this time sending themselves up), featuring regularly in *Viz* magazine and, for Janette, the opportunity to star alongside Oscar-winner Julie Walters in the BBC series *Dinner Ladies* and in the 2003 series of *Absolutely Fabulous*.

The cameras also followed them once again for the documentary series *The Entertainers* while they became regulars on the chat-show circuit, appearing on Frank Skinner and Jonathan Ross's programmes where they would, as usual, be relentlessly quizzed about their 'curious' relationship.

Now, in their autobiography, they reveal in their own words the truth about their remarkable careers – spanning five decades – and their incredible marriage.

And they explain that since tying the knot in 1969 they have always been together – although they weren't always faithful to each other …

1

THE TOUGHS GET GOING

Janette

I was born on 16 May 1947 and christened Janet Anderson, but because my granny was also a Janet they called me Janette. I lived in a council house in Mill Road, Queenzieburn, beside Kilsyth on the outskirts of Glasgow and was an only child. My father was William Anderson from Kirkintilloch – he was a miner all his life and was himself an only child – but my mum Mary Kelly, who worked in an ammunition factory during the war, was one of ten. Dad had actually been married before, to a nurse who tragically died in childbirth, while the twins she was delivering sadly died too. I didn't find that out until I was 23. But although he had been married before, Mum and Dad were completely dedicated to each other.

I had a lovely childhood, attending Chapel Green Primary School. Although I was 8lb when I was born, I was always small, even when I went to school, and became the smallest there. I always remember that I was so small my wee legs

1

wouldn't reach the floor, even in the smallest Primary One seats. I was perfectly in proportion, just tiny. I was a perfectly healthy baby and child. When I was about three, the doctors said I wasn't growing very much. But back then they just said, 'This is going to be a small one,' as there was nothing else they could do.

When I went to school, one of the nurses who used to come around – you know, a Nitty Nora the Head Explorer – decided to find out why I was so tiny. She sent me to Yorkhill Hospital when I was about six. They did loads of tests on me and eventually gave me a clean bill of health. Nowadays, they would have given me growth hormones, but not in the 1950s. There's no condition or anything to label me with. I'm just small. All the boys at school used to call me 'the giant', which was funny. They'd say, 'Oh, here's the giant coming ...' They weren't bullies, they were just cheeky, and I was never bullied at all.

I actually kept growing until I was 16, just at about a third of the rate of everyone else, and stopped when I reached 4ft 5in.

When I went to Kilsyth Academy, I was, of course, the smallest yet again. I loved the Academy and ended up taking a language and commercial course, doing shorthand, typing and bookkeeping. All the kids actually voted me Class Captain. I don't think it was a sympathy vote because I talked to everyone, always have, so I was friendly and knew them all. I didn't dislike many people, and that's continued right through my whole life. I also went to Girl Guides and Sunday School and was a Patrol Leader, being in charge of the tents when we went camping. I had to sleep at the front of the tent and be in charge of these great big lassies – *me* protecting *them*! It looked like I had thousands of badges because my arms were so short.

I got the performing bug when I was three. We went on a family holiday to the Isle of Man and there was music playing on the boat. My dad had one of those Brownie cameras and took pictures of me dancing away in front of all the passengers. The funny thing was I was doing proper dance steps like a ballerina. I think everyone was amazed.

When I was seven, I started dancing lessons. I went to Georgie Grey School of Dancing in Kirkintilloch. The classes were held in a little hut on the canal bank. It was two shillings for a tap lesson or two and six for a ballet lesson on a Saturday morning. I did both. All the other kids were taller than me, of course, which meant they could never match me up with anyone for the routines so I always got the solo part. I did my first concert at Kirkintilloch Town Hall at seven where I sang the song 'Bimbo'. The ironic thing about that is I had to wear a little boy's outfit, with a red cap, just like Jimmy Krankie would wear all those years later. It was the dancing teacher's idea, so she got me shorts, red cap and a bow-tie – if only she knew what she was about to start!

As soon as I put the outfit on, I found it really easy to be a wee boy. No problems at all, which was amazing because I wasn't a tomboy at all. I was a cute, wee girlie.

At school, the only real trouble I had was from a teacher called Miss Hall when we had to do typing. The typewriter was too high for me. She wouldn't give me a cushion to sit on; instead, she would make me take a drawer out of her desk, turn it upside down and I had to sit on that. Of course, the underside of the drawer was just rough wood so it would give me splinters in my legs. I said to her, 'Miss Hall, this drawer is hurting my legs.' All she gave me was a yellow duster to put on top of it. I remember one day the drawer slipped off the seat and I went through the drawer, and I got into a row for breaking it – compassion was never one of her strong points.

I was an average student but, like everyone, I got belted. It was always for talking, although it wasn't for cheeking the teachers back. You'd get belted for having a sweet, belted for yawning … they belted you for everything back then. But I finally left school at 16 with a commercial certificate and went for a few job interviews.

I had kept up my dancing during all that time and would entertain pensioners at old folks' homes in my spare time. I got turned down for a couple of jobs at the bank and council offices in Kirkintilloch. It could have been down to my height because they certainly weren't equal-opportunities employers then. I then spotted an advert in the paper for a junior clerk for a company called Reliance Telephones in North Street, Glasgow. My mum came with me for the interview and I got that job. I started off filing, but I was so small I couldn't reach the top files, so they got me a little set of steps. When I was filing, I was always singing away. There was a salesman in the office called Ron Robson who was married to Anne Fields, who was the cousin of the late Jimmy Logan.

Ron had been in a band called The Jones Boys in the 1950s, so he had had a great deal of experience in showbiz. He was the first person who ever said to me, 'Have you ever thought of being in showbusiness?' I didn't even know what he was talking about. He said, 'Well, my wife is in showbusiness, her name is Anne Fields and I think you would also be great in showbusiness too.' He then told me about a panto that was coming up called *The World of Widow Krankie* with Jack Milroy at The Pavilion. There were roles for six children but they didn't want to use kids because of some licensing laws. He then said that he was going to come out to Queenzieburn and have a little chat with my mum and dad.

Well, he rolled up outside our little council house in a great big blue Jaguar. My mother was beside herself and had the best china out for Ron and Anne coming to the house. Anne just looked like a star – fur coat, blonde hair, sheer elegance and my mum simply loved her. They both had a chat with my parents and asked if they could take me for an audition to the Gaiety Theatre in Ayr and thankfully Mum and Dad said, 'Yes!'

I remember my first audition as if it was yesterday. I sang 'Baby Face', did a tap dance and I've been in the business ever since. I will also never forget my first wage from entertainment. I did 13 shows a week for 10 shillings a show – £6 10s a week. At the office, I was on £3 10s a week, so with both jobs I had effectively tripled my wages. I was leaving Queenzieburn on the 7.45am bus, working at the office until 5.15pm, and then straight down to The Pavilion Theatre to do a 6.10pm and 8.40pm show, before rushing to get the last bus home – only to get up and do it all over again the next day.

I used to give my mum £3 digs money and I saved everything else, although I did splash out on a few luxuries.

The first was a white rabbit-skin fur coat, which I bought from Frasers – children's size, of course – and it cost me a whopping £30, a hell of a lot of money back then.

I did three years with the famous Scottish entertainer Jack Milroy in *The World of Widow Krankie* then *Widow Krankie's Hanky Panky* and then *Carry On Krankie*. I got on well with Jack. Years later, when I got very friendly with him, he came out on our boat and asked me, 'How much did I pay you when you started out?' I told him £6 10s and he berated himself, saying, 'That was helluva mean.' But I loved the man to death and he was a great inspiration for my facial expressions.

One of Jack's big strengths was that he could get a laugh with any tame little gag with just a facial expression. That is very akin to Scottish comics. Lex McLean was the same. Other people would set up the jokes and Lex would knock the crowd dead just by pulling a face. So I'd watch everything Jack would do and I remember noting that the biggest laughs came from his face – he got more laughs from that than from someone who just stood there telling jokes. It's something I'd end up using all my career.

Things always used to happen to me in the show. I would trip over my nightie on stage when all the Widow's kids were getting out of bed and I'd be told to 'keep that in' because it got a laugh. Jack encouraged me all the time and would include me in sketches too.

I kept up both jobs for two years, but was so exhausted I thought I couldn't do it any more. I was then offered my first summer season, which meant, combined with the panto, I could afford to go professional. So, in 1963, I gave up the office for showbiz.

I never had many dreams and ambitions in my head at the time to be truthful. I am very much a live-for-the-day type of person. I still don't really plan for the future. If I'm doing a show then I've got to concentrate on that one thing only; I can't be thinking of lots of other things like 'What does it all mean?' and 'Why are we put on the earth?' That's all too complicated and stressful, so I just think what will I do for the rest of the day when I wake up in the morning and little else.

During the summer season with Jack, one of the musicians suggested to me and another Krankie kid, Margaret Murray, that we should get our own act together and try our luck at performing in the clubs in Manchester. It made sense because we had a break before panto started up again. He gave us some names of agents and we sent pictures of ourselves in little silver outfits wearing mini-skirts and silver caps. I always remember when I left home for Manchester when I was 18, my mum and dad got me to the Buchanan Street bus station and cried their eyes out. But they never once tried to stop me. Not once in my life did they attempt to put the blocks on what I was doing. However, I never took advantage of them and they always trusted me.

We found digs at Rosie Dylan's guesthouse. Rosie was an old Irish woman with teeth like a row of condemned buildings, but she was a great person. Sometimes, we'd get in from gigs at 2.00am and Rosie would leave us parcels of sandwiches with our names on them. If the musicians got in first, though, then your sandwiches – with your name on them or not – would be gone.

Margaret and I would be doing the clubs, performing solo

spots then teaming up together to do a bit of Scottish stuff, dancing and that kind of thing. We called ourselves The Krankie Kids. We originally went down to Manchester for a fortnight and stayed 12 weeks.

The clubs were pretty seedy. One night, the booker told us we'd be sharing the bill with 32 strippers and he wanted to put us on as a novelty act. He asked if we'd mind if he changed our name on the billing to The Kinky Kids. So there was prim-and-proper Margaret and I sitting in this crowded dressing room with our matching blue cases surrounded by 32 naked strippers. One of the strippers said to me, 'Can I borrow your lipstick, love?'

'Sure,' I replied.

The next second, she had lifted up her top and painted her nipples with my lipstick and went to hand me it back. I said, 'It's all right, you can keep it.' All this time I would be writing home telling my mum everything was going fine. If only she knew!

The drag queens, strippers and comics were actually very protective of us and would walk us to the bus stop at midnight to make sure we got home all right. But Margaret and I loved it. The whole experience completely opened the eyes of this wee girl from Queenzieburn. My family were never drinkers, but suddenly I was able to enjoy a wee tipple. But we were never promiscuous or anything like that, even though I did end up with a boyfriend.

* * *

Ian

I was born Ian Robert Tough on 26 March 1947, into quite a privileged family of Clydebank butchers. I am the middle son of three – Alistair is two years my senior while Colin is 13 years my junior – and was delivered into the world in a private nursing home in Glasgow's Great Western Road.

The family business had been started by my grandfather Robert, whose slogan was 'If it's Toughs, it's tender', before my dad Alex and uncle Bobby took over the reins.

My mother is originally from Manchester and met my dad when she moved up to Glasgow. My dad was a butcher during the week and a football player at the weekends, playing outside-left for Ayr Utd.

We were actually better off than a lot of people at the time because my grandfather had won £14,000 on the Pools in 1947 – which was a fortune back then. I never knew this until years later and I suppose it could explain our smart bungalow at 56 Drumry Road, the reason I was born in a private nursing home and my dad's new cars!

I was very ill when I was born with a condition that 16 years later would change the course of my life. I had lumps growing under my skin and spent the first six months in the Sick Children's Hospital. No one knew what was wrong with me. The doctors thought it was some sort of blood disorder and put me on a new drug, penicillin, and it seemed to cure me.

But when I was 16 I took very ill and nearly died. The surgeons removed my spleen as they discovered I had a diversion in my blood system – basically, my blood was coursing around my body the wrong way. That was the defining moment that actually got me into showbusiness because, at the time, I was an apprentice electrician and I couldn't do the heavy work after I left hospital.

At school, I had been an average student. I was intelligent enough but I hated school ... every minute of it. I attended Radnor Park, which ended up being condemned as they still had a bomb crater in the middle of the playground from the Clydebank Blitz, so we were moved to Kilbowie and then Braidfield Secondary.

I was a wild boy, wild all the time. I was hyperactive. I remember when I was four I'd been so bad that, for punishment, my aunt Jessie, who worked in the shop, stripped me down to my underpants and put me in the butcher shop's window with a 'For Sale' sign around my neck. When I was nine, I smashed ten windows in a local catholic school and broke four statues – but got caught. I also bit the school janitor who caught me. My dad was actually the local magistrate. There were no Children's Panels back then for me to be hauled before, and I was too young to be charged, so I'd get walloped by my dad, practically every night, but it made no difference whatsoever.

At ten, I was up to all sorts and even burned down our own garden shed. My parents didn't even need to ask, they knew it was me.

Surprisingly, though, I could always make them laugh. They had to laugh or they'd cry. It was a case of 'Oh no, what's he done now?' The laughter probably saved their sanity. I honestly never set out to do bad things. I just didn't think, not once ... I just did it.

I was raised as a Protestant and I was made aware when I went to Kilbowie Church every Sunday that I wasn't supposed to have Catholic friends. That's how backwards it was then – it still is, sadly, in parts of Scotland today. It was very strange when Janette and I moved to England years later when we discovered people weren't bothered what faith you were born into. I liked that.

During my tearaway years, I had an aunt Grace – a maiden aunt who never married – who was worried sick about me and told my parents I was hyperactive. She was an actress in the Clydebank Rep so she took me down to acting school. That's where I met Barbara Rafferty for the first time, who went on to find fame as Ella Cotter in *Rab C Nesbitt* on television. We were in a play together. I also met James Cosmo, who went on to star as Mel Gibson's sidekick in *Braveheart* and appeared in a host of other movies. He was younger than me but was always a big, tall bugger and towered above the rest of us. I always remember he was really ambitious; even back then, he'd tell us he was going to be a big actor, and he certainly became a big actor in more ways than one and good luck to him.

I loved acting primarily because I was showing off. I never had any nerves or stage fright or anything like that. I would just get out there and everyone paid attention to me – perfect. My grampa regularly took me to the Alhambra Theatre in Glasgow. I loved being inside a real theatre. I'll never forget how excited I'd be at the weekend, knowing I was going there.

Although I found an outlet on stage, I never lost that nasty streak, which stayed with me right through to adulthood. As a young man, I always tended to be a bit quick with my fists, especially if someone insulted Janette for her height. I remember in Sheffield we were walking down the street when someone shouted something like, 'Look at that short-arse ...' – I just went for him. Janette hated that and she actually warned me if I did that again she would leave me, because she couldn't stand it any longer.

It was the same when I was younger. I would actually batter guys older than me if they tried to pick on my big brother; I would nearly kill them. Alistair was a bookworm so some of the rough lads would have a go, but not if I was around.

When I went to the Theatre Guild at 14, that was the first time in my life I appreciated, there were gay people in the world. This one guy called Robert Love, who was also in the Guild, had said to my dad that he would keep an eye on me and nothing would happen – he was true to his word, everyone was nothing but nice to me. At this point, I had left school and was doing an apprenticeship at James Scott and Company.

Scott's was an electrical engineers. I ended up in there after I'd gone to see the guidance teacher at school. All the boys would queue up and they'd tell you 'Right, you're going to the shipyards, you're going Singers Sewing Machines', but when I said my name, this teacher said, 'Well, your family are butchers, so you're going to be a butcher too.' I was like, 'I'm not going to be a butcher,' so he said, 'Right then, the corset factory.'

I told him there was no way I was going to work in a corset factory and my dad would sort everything out, which made the teacher pretty irate. My dad knew the personnel manager at James Scott and got me in the door.

I left school at 15 because I was constantly beaten at Braidfield with a strap. They'd belt me for everything. I'd get walloped if I walked two paces faster than the art teacher on the way to class. When I look back on it, I'm sure they were picking on me ... every bloody day! I just could not resist cheeking them back. Then, of course, the rest of the class would kill themselves laughing and that just made me worse. So it was worth the pain. But when I'd go home, my dad – who was an army man and a strict disciplinarian – would check to see if I had any marks on my wrists and if I did he'd belt me too. So, basically, I was belted constantly at home and at school. Today, they'd be jailed, but that's just the way it was back then.

So the only qualification I left with was a certificate in cycling proficiency – no kidding.

At James Scott and Company in Finneston I worked as a store boy and had to get up at 6.00am for work. Just two hours into my first day on the job, I realised what a bloody mistake I'd made. It was hard work. The gaffers in there were worse than the school teachers, and far more frightening. They were big, rough men, who'd belt you around the ear and make you do stupid things – all the usual stuff apprentices had to go through ... go and find a left-handed screwdriver and all that rubbish. Over the months, though, I gradually got to like it and these rough bastards got to like me.

But when I was 16, after a day on a building site in Knightswood, I took ill when I got home that night. I was always an anaemic-looking kid and dead skinny, not stocky like I am now. I had blood tests and something came up. The doctors kept asking if I'd ever been to Africa because I had all the symptoms of Yellow Fever – but I hadn't been out of Clydebank, never mind Scotland. Then they thought it may be blood cancer before discovering I had an enlarged spleen, which they decided to remove. I'd probably aggravated things as I was doing heavy work that day, cycled home, cut the grass and drunk two bottles of fizzy drink, which was about the worst thing I could have done. I was sick on the spot and spewed up blood.

I was rushed to the Western Infirmary where they called for the minister because they thought I wasn't going to make it. I have a rare blood group – type B rhesus negative. Fortunately, my brother Alistair has the same so he was hooked up to give me a few pints. That probably saved me. Years later, I was told that I had been born a 'blue baby', which meant I should have had a total blood transfusion at birth, but they had missed it, or just hadn't known in 1947.

I was in hospital for 16 weeks until they got the bleeding in my stomach to stop. They actually put a balloon into my stomach and inflated it to stop the haemorrhaging. It worked. The blood had been going the wrong way and was contaminating itself with toxins. I still wasn't out of the woods yet because I contracted pneumonia three times after that.

The doctors told me that I couldn't go back to heavy lifting again. James Scott were very good and said they'd retrain me as an electrician and would give me lighter work, and I wouldn't have to go out on the building sites. In the meantime, I was back in amateur dramatics and did a production of *Guys and Dolls* when I was 17 playing Liver Lips Louis.

I loved the musicals and before *Guys and Dolls* I'd been in *Charlie's Aunt* and *No No Nanette*.

The electrical manager at The Pavilion Theatre at the time was always pissed and the stage manager Ian Gillespie kept saying that he would have to get rid of him. Being a chancer, I told Ian that I could do that job. I was desperate to get into the theatre permanently. At the time, I was fitting ships down on the dockyards and seeing guys who looked 60 but were only in their 40s. They'd be out in the worst weather with their welding gear, freezing their bollocks off in the snow, and I just couldn't wait to get to The Pavilion when work finished. I loved the buzz of the theatre. I liked the people. There were all sorts – gay, straight, swingers – but they were all 'softer' people. They'd talk about *The Stage* newspaper and it was a completely different world, and I longed to be a part of it.

So I started off as the light boy, then this old electrician got so bad – he would be steaming at work – that they finally got rid of him. The proprietor asked me if I could do the job of chief electrician and I bluffed it and said that I had my City and Guilds qualifications, which was total bollocks. I didn't dare tell my dad that I had chucked James Scott for two weeks. I would still get up at 6.00am and pretend I was going to work and would sit in a café in Glasgow's George Square until the theatre opened at 10.00am. I thought I was on easy street until the manager Mr Docherty informed me one day that Mr Balantyne the proprietor wanted to rewire the entire theatre and needed to know if his new chief electrician – me – who was completely unqualified in anything whatsoever, could manage this mammoth task. I was to start with the backstage area, which was in a complete mess. However, it just so happened that I had made friends with the foreman at an electrical company in Sauchiehall Street. I rushed up to him and said, 'I'm really in the shit here … they want The

Pavilion rewired and I can't do it.' He just laughed and said he would help. I promised him £10 a week and, thankfully, he did the lot. He rewired the entire theatre with me as his lackey, and installed a brand-new, state-of-the-art operations board too. It was magnificent and no one at The Pavilion was any the wiser. This real sparky then taught me how to work the new board.

On the night of The Pavilion relaunch, which was *The Lex McLean Show*, I said to the boss, 'Now, I have to have a word with you, Mr Docherty … I'm doing a lot of work here and I'm still only getting £9 a week – and I want a raise.' He told me to piss off and I said, 'Fine, I'll get a job at the King's Theatre now, because I'm the only person in Scotland who can work this new board.' He realised I had him by the short and curlies, so I got a raise on the spot.

2

PUTTING ON AN ACT

Janette

Margaret and I had moved to another guesthouse in Manchester to be nearer the clubs when Jack, a Canadian solider, turned up. He was quite tall and we were instantly attracted to each other, although we didn't have sex or anything like that – just snogging. He was my first boyfriend. He was always talking about taking me over to Canada but we broke up when I returned to panto at The Pavilion in *Goosey Goosey Glasgow* with Johnny Beattie in 1965. That was the first time I met Ian but, lo and behold, the Canadian turned up unannounced at my house at New Year. He was just a few weeks too late because I had started going out with Ian just before Christmas. So when he arrived, I had no interest in him. But my mum felt sorry for him and I will never forget that the poor bugger had to sleep in my dad's caravan in the back garden in the freezing cold. I bet he wished he'd gone back to Canada instead of chasing me to Queenzieburn.

I met Ian while playing Johnny Beattie's daughter Jinty during the panto.

Ian was quite a smart and tidy wee boy. He always smelled of nice aftershave, which was very unusual for The Pavilion stage crew at the time, believe me. He had Merrymaid caramels and used to throw these sweets at me on stage from the lightbox. I hated caramels but I would take them anyway – I'm sure there are names for people like him handing out sweeties to little girls.

He then asked me out and we went to the pictures. Afterwards, we went for a Chinese meal. Ian had paid for the cinema but I paid for the Chinese because I was on more money than him earning £9 a week, while Ian was on £6 10s a week.

Ian's dad had a Ford Cortina, which we used to borrow on a Sunday and go for a drive up to Fintry and have a meal at The Covenanters pub. But the funny thing was that Ian only got the car every alternate Sunday as he had to share it with his older brother Alistair. Sometimes, when we were snogging, we'd find a pair of knickers under the seat from Alistair's last date the weekend before. My favourite white-rabbit fur coat would always come off over Ian's smart suits, so people always knew what we'd been up to.

Ian

My randy brother started dating Jean Ambler from the chorus line – and ended up marrying her. Alistair and Jean are still together today.

But I was only throwing toffees at Janette because I fancied her rotten and also because I honestly thought she was the major talent of the show – however sickly that sounds, it's true. She was just a different class and I'd never seen anything like her with all the visiting shows and acts that came in. Janette had charisma. She would have that Glasgow crowd in her hand and that's what I call true star quality.

At the time, I was still seeing a girl called Irene McCann, who was a secretary at Scottish Opera. She was the total opposite from me and was very posh and sophisticated, or 'arty farty' as I would say. I think we were both getting fed up with each other. She took me once to see some opera with all her luvvie-dovey mob, but I went to the bar and got absolutely pished and made a complete arse of myself. I think I started heckling the singers, that was after stumbling over half the audience while coming back to my seat late. That was my first and last experience of opera.

After I asked Janette out on the Friday, the act The Dallas Boys from the show then suggested that we should all go skiing on the Sunday up at Glen Shee. We didn't have ski gear or anything like that and were wearing our denims. I ended up skiing backwards into a burn and Janette had to help me dry off in the bus, holding my towel; I was bloody frozen. Janette at the time had taken a wee shine to my older brother Alistair, but after that day's skiing we hit it off – she obviously liked what she saw behind that towel, even though it was freezing cold.

Janette

I fancied Ian's brother because, on a Saturday matinée, he used to come in and help change the scenery and I thought he was a bit of all right. He was even smoother than Ian. But we never went out as things developed with Ian after the ski trip. In fact, on the way back on the bus, Ian ended up singing something from *West Side Story* and I realised that he had a great voice; that's when he told me he'd been in amateur dramatics. To be honest, it wasn't some huge big love-at-first-sight scenario. It was a gradual thing that we grew to really like each other.

After panto, I was asked to go to Edinburgh with Jack Milroy for the summer but, because I'd been to Manchester the year before, I had a hunch that the showbiz scene was changing more into the clubs and cabaret.

Ian

Janette had told me that things were changing so that's when we decided to get our own act together and we'd rehearse at Kilbowie Church Hall. We didn't really have a clue what we were going to do. I would open with a Sinatra song and I'd do stand-up before we started doing comedy together using props. Our first gig together was at The Strand in Glasgow, which was cabaret acts with a compere. We went on as 'Jinty and Tough'. The best I can say is that we were OK. Although it wasn't a particularly memorable occasion, Jack Short – who was Jimmy Logan's father – said to us afterwards, 'I've got a big charity show on at the Metropole,' and he put us on. We did comedy lines to link songs and Janette danced.

Janette

We didn't have a structure to our show and didn't know where we were going, but somehow we stumbled our way through the performance at the Metropole, and although we didn't exactly set the heather on fire, we hadn't embarrassed ourselves. The only other gig we did in Glasgow was at Ian's mum and dad's silver wedding anniversary and that was it.

We would return to do the occasional club in Scotland in the mid-1970s. But it was never one of our main stomping grounds. We'd only do a week at the most every year. We met a bingo-hall owner Ronnie Nesbitt in Jersey in 1975 who told us his bingo was falling away and he wanted to put us on doing cabaret. So we were booked to do the Mecca Bingo in Partick and in the Gorbals back in Glasgow.

Ian

For part of our act Janette used to dress up as a Womble. But to come in as a Womble, she had to go out a side door of the building, on to the street and come back in through the bingo hall.

Janette

As I was doing this in my full Womble costume, I ran past this drunk in the street, who had stopped in his tracks and was staring at me bleary eyed. I just ran past him and never thought anything more of it. But our musical director Davie was having a pint and told us later that a man ran into the pub and said to the barmaid, 'Oh Jesus, geeze a large whisky …' She was like, 'What's the matter?' And he said, 'I just saw this bloody big rat running into the bingo hall – honest to God it was about 4ft high.' Needless to say, everyone in the bar just thought he'd had too much to drink.

Ian

In the Gorbals, I was setting up my speakers on stage long

before the show and there were four wee, hard Glaswegian women sitting at a table down below. With typical Glaswegian tact, one of them shouted, 'Oy, son, whit are ye daein?'

'I'm setting up my speakers – I'm the cabaret tonight,' I replied.

'Cabaret?' she shouted, 'Cabaret? Are you any bloody good?'

Quick as a flash, I replied, 'If I was any bloody good I wouldn't be here.'

She thought about it for a second and said, 'Aye, you've got a point there, son.'

Janette

Back then, we knew we had a lot to learn and, in June of 1966, Ian and I headed to Manchester to work in the clubs. My mum and dad didn't have a problem with me going off with Ian as they really liked him. Ian actually got more hassle from his family than I did.

Ian

We felt we had to move because Scotland at the time was a closed shop and the showbusiness scene was run by just a handful of people. It was very hard to break through, especially doing what we were trying to do. So, really, we took a gamble and went south.

When I'd left for Manchester, an aunt heard I'd gone with Janette and said to my father, 'You shall go down there and drag him back up here.' She called me a disgrace to the family. Fortunately, it didn't come to that. It's amazing because that attitude wasn't really so long ago. Look how quickly the world and attitudes have changed.

When we got to Manchester, old Rosie Dylan wouldn't let us share a room together in her B&B unless we were married. So much for the Swinging Sixties.

Janette

The agent I had worked for previously got us gigs again, some of them in horrendous places. I remember one – the Del Sol – which was a real dive with black-and-white tiles; the place looked like a lavatory. It didn't open until 1.00am. We would do 14 shows a week for this agent and were on £6 a show, making £12 a night. Out of that we had to pay digs and the agent's fee, but we were still clearing £50 a week – the average wage in Britain was £12 a week at the time.

Ian

To be honest, Manchester was too soon for us. The massive old English pubs were fine, but the clubs were a disaster as we were doing the hell-holes. It was the era of the smoky jazz-playing musicians in these big casinos. Then we came in singing 'Open Up Those Pearly Gates' and that kind of shit – it didn't go down well at all.

There were also some really heavy characters. There was one venue called Mr Smith's and the first night we were on there were only five people in the crowd. I jokingly said to him, 'How will you be able to afford us tonight?' He looked me in the eye and said, 'Well, on Saturday night you'll come back here and gamble and I shall get all my money back.' I naïvely said, 'But we don't gamble.' And he replied, 'You do now.'

Janette

An Italian manager at a club came up to us when we'd just started the act and said, 'No, no, no … you're like a couple of Salvation Army children – I'm going to get rid of you,' and he sacked us on the opening night.

Even though it could be rough, we still liked the buzz of the clubs because we were just 20 years old. We were so happy just being together that we didn't mind the rough nights with these dodgy characters. We were of the opinion 'tomorrow's another day'. We also firmly believed that our act would get better. Put it this way … it couldn't get any worse.

Another act called The Two Gerrards from Hull were also staying in the same guesthouse as us. They were a real old-style variety act. She used to come down in the morning in full make-up, including blue eye-shadow and false eyelashes. She was also always stinking of Avon perfume that caught the back of your throat so much it was an effort to eat your breakfast. The other half of the act was Maori. But they suggested that we should come to Hull to start somewhere smaller to help develop our act. They were kind enough to put us up for three weeks before we got our own place in Hull. We rented a flat for £4 a week but, again, we couldn't tell the landlady that we weren't married so we pretended we were brother and sister.

There was no phone or anything and Ian would use the phonebox across the road as his own personal office. We were struggling badly for money at the time. Next door to us was a young teacher, who was quite 'New Age', and would smoke dope and that sort of thing. I remember one day we didn't have any money for coal and we were absolutely freezing. Ian had gone out and found this piece of fencing and chopped it up to light the fire and then we went to bed to keep warm.

Ian

We also discovered that plenty of bonking was the best way to keep warm. But that didn't stop us from being hungry, so I actually used to go next door into this hippy teacher's garden and steal her cabbages during the day when she was at school. I also dug up her potatoes and carrots; believe me, we were that desperate.

Janette

After we got a few more gigs, we decided to invest in our first car so we could travel further for work. We bought this Vauxhall Victor for £60. It was maroon, apart from a grey driver's door. We eventually got a week's work in the Spennymore Variety Club, Co. Durham. But our car broke down driving from Hull to Leeds. We had to be there at 11.00am for the lunchtime show. The other problem was that, before the trip, we didn't even have enough fuel to get all the way there, so I had to pawn our radio just so we could fill the car up. When we broke down, it was so cold I thought we were going to die from hypothermia. We managed to find a garage and explained our problem to the mechanic; he repaired it for nothing and we were able to get to our gig, where we slept in the car park waiting for the venue to open.

On the second night, when we were driving to the gig, the car skidded on ice and we actually somersaulted three times. It seemed to last for ever. In those days, there weren't any seatbelts and it was just bench seats, so we ended up sitting on the roof of the car. One of the other acts on the bill, Bobby Jean and the Scot Boys, were behind us. Amazingly, we were unscathed, just a little dizzy, and Bobby Jean drove us on to the gig where we did our show.

Our old Vauxhall Victor was a write-off, though, so the next night Bobby Jean drove us to the gig and he ended up skidding and hit a wall. So I told Ian we're not opening our act with 'Open Up Those Pearly Gates' ever again.

Ian

We were dazed and confused after that first crash, but didn't want to lose the work, so we didn't even think about cancelling.

The working men's clubs were much better venues for us though. They were busier for a start, and people wanted to be entertained instead of being there to gamble.

Janette

We started using more visual props too, and doing more chart songs like Rolf Harris's 'Tie My Kangaroo Down'. I would use a giant wobble board, which you couldn't see me behind until I popped my head up.

By the summer of 1967, the work had dried up, and I called Bob Johnson, a contact I'd met on my first stint in Manchester with Margaret. Bob was now working in Wiesbaden in Germany as the agent providing the Forces entertainment and he gave us two months' work in the American bases. The two of us didn't have passports, nor had we even been out of the country, but suddenly we were destined for Germany and, after hastily getting our documents in order, jumped on the train.

By this time, we had all these props like the wobble board, a giant Mexican sombrero and huge bass drum, so we got off the train in Wiesbaden at 6.00am and promptly got arrested.

Ian

The police in this posh little place were all for running us out of town. We had stepped off our train with all our props and were immediately pounced on by two cops. They obviously thought we were a couple of vagabonds and they just started bawling at us, asking for our permits – or that's what it sounded like, anyway – and I remember thinking to myself, 'This is some welcoming committee.' Fortunately, one of their superiors, who spoke English, turned up and, after we explained, he apologised for the other two officers' behaviour and escorted us to our hotel.

Janette

It was a huge place. It was the first time we'd ever seen duvets. Big puffy things, they were beautiful, and we couldn't stop rolling about in them.

Ian

But the big *fräulein* manageress used to give me terrible looks because she knew Janette and I were sharing a room and she thought Janette was just a little girl. So she had me pegged as some sort of pervert. Every morning she'd pat Janette on the head then scowl at me.

Janette

It was only when I had my 21st birthday at the hotel did she finally believe I wasn't a little girl and stopped giving me sweeties every morning.

Ian

Our contact in Germany was Charlie Koch, who was a black Jewish agent from Miami. What we never realised was that we were entertaining American kids on their way to Vietnam. And when we moved to Turkey a few months later to their bases there, we were performing to kids on their way back. They were just our age. It was tragic.

We worked with an American comic juggler called Terry Bergen. He said to us, 'You guys are talking all wrong.' We were never bolshy bastards and would always listen to people – something that I find the young acts of today simply don't do. Terry taught us the basics, such as saying 'the sidewalk' instead of 'the pavement' and 'the trunk' and not 'the boot' of a car. He also told us not to be frightened to talk back to the GIs as they'd be shouting at us on stage. We'd never come across anything like that before where the audience actually shouted at you. He taught us some put- downs for the hecklers as well, such as, 'Why don't you stand next to the wall, buddy, it's plastered too?' It worked. If you knocked them down, they loved you.

Janette

We would do things like sing parodies of *The Sound of Music*, which was out at the time

'I'm just 16, going on 17 … one day I'll reach two feet …'
The Yanks loved all that stuff.

Ian

We were getting paid £80 a week, plus our travel – an absolute fortune. But we certainly earned our money when we went to Turkey. That was simply horrendous.

Janette

On the bill with us in the show was a vent act called Terri Rogers who had had a sex change. Now Ian and I had never even heard the term 'sex change' before. But this fella had had all his bits cut off. On top of this, she was now a ventriloquist – the best we've ever seen. Her doll was called Bobby Kimba.

Ian

It turned out this guy had been a merchant seaman called Bobby Kimba who changed his name to Terri Rogers after having his sex change, but gave his doll his old name.

Janette

We went to Istanbul first and then travelled through the deserts in a Volkswagen van with Terri and a singing act called Michelle and Miles from Leeds. When we got to the Black Sea, Michelle and I went down to the beach. Terri came too, but always wore a skirted bathing suit, and Michelle and I would try to look up it to see if she had a willy. She had boobs and everything, but when we travelled overnight in the van, by the next morning Terri would have a five o'clock shadow.

Ian

We got to this God-forsaken place in the middle of Turkey and arrived at the hotel reception, which was full of all these Turks in their traditional clothes, smoking pipes, and Terri actually made the phone ring across the other side of the room by throwing her voice. She then did card tricks for them and they were absolutely fascinated by her. That is until after the gig when we were getting in the van and we were pelted with bricks. A huge gang of Turks had gathered and were trying to attack Terri. They thought she was a witch and wanted to kill her. Even the police were after her. Of course, the bloody van wouldn't start and the crowd were swaying it back and forth trying to overturn us. We thought the worst. Suddenly, it burst into life and we shot off through this sheep market, where the animals and the farmers literally had to jump out of our way as we escaped.

Janette

We would be eating in these awful cafés in the middle of nowhere. They'd be cooking things up in what looked like giant dustbins and we didn't have a clue what we were actually eating, but we were starving and had no choice. The food actually tasted beautiful, but it was guaranteed, no mattered how tasty it was or where you ate, six hours later we'd all get the trots. It was pretty hard going having the trots while travelling in a van over bumpy roads in the searing heat.

Ian

Having the runs was awful. It was so bad I was scared to fart. What's more, on the roads we were travelling there'd be rock falls, so quite often we had to get out and shift boulders just to continue – while all the time we were in severe danger of shitting ourselves!

Fortunately, we ate really well in the American bases themselves. I had never seen a T-bone steak until I arrived there. I couldn't believe that one person could eat so much meat.

Janette

On one occasion, our van broke down and we had to get on the public bus with all our props and gear. All the locals would be sitting in silence staring at us. I swear this is true – the bus actually stopped at a field and two sheep got on. Just two sheep, no shepherd or anything. No one else on the bus batted an eyelid. We drove ten miles down the road, stopped, and the sheep got off without any encouragement at all. I'd never seen anything like it. Ian then leaned over to me and said, 'You know when we go to get off this bus, there'll probably be a pig driving it.'

Ian

We didn't even know where we were going or where we were. We ended up on the Iraq border one day, so we could have performed to a young Saddam Hussein for all we know.

Janette

But at the end of our tour, we got engaged. Ian bought me a diamond ring from a jeweller's in Istanbul and we got engaged on the boat crossing the Bosporus between Europe and Asia in June 1968.

Ian

It was probably the first and *last* romantic thing I've done in my life.

Janette

The only snag was, about six months later, when we were back home I was looking at my ring when I said to Ian, 'My diamond's cracked.' He was like, 'A diamond canny crack …' We took it to a local jeweller's who told us it was just a piece of glass over solder. So Ian had been well and truly conned out of his £25.

We'd come back to Scotland to tell our parents we'd got engaged. My parents were delighted. They adored Ian. If I used to shout at Ian in the house, my mum would shout at me for ticking him off.

Ian

Mine weren't so happy, not because of Janette but because they were still worried about what I was doing in my life and because I didn't have a 'proper job'.

Janette

We were then offered another tour of Turkey for the following year. After a fortnight, you forget all the bad stuff because you're young and it was all one big adventure, so we agreed.

Ian

The train we took this time from Germany to Turkey was the original *Orient Express*. But the luxury seating had been replaced by 12 inches of wooden slatted chairs. It got so hot we got sweat rashes.

One day, we were stopped on the Bulgarian border. This was in the days of Communism where the police woke you up by banging their guns on your arms. They ordered the transvestite Terri to bring her suitcase down, which had her ventriloquist dummy inside, and she started throwing her voice to make it sound as if someone was trapped inside. Then she would open the case a little and 'the voice' would get louder.

This policeman poked her case with his gun, then a big smile crept across his face. He loved her. He then asked where we were going and when we said we were going to entertain the Americans, he said, 'No, you will entertain us.' He threatened to drag us all off the train so we could perform for the police. Fortunately, we managed to talk our way out of it.

Janette
When we returned to England, we got rid of the Hull flat and decided we'd live in the middle of the country so it was easier to travel. So we moved to Nottingham, then contacted an agent, Jack Derman, and started doing clubs in the Midlands.

Ian
Being in Germany and Turkey had given us a lot more confidence and we were definitely getting better. It was also great to be playing a crowd once again where we weren't constantly having to fight the audience like we had to do with the Yanks.

Janette
We would do a lot of things called Shop Windows in the working men's clubs, where we'd perform not only in front

of the audience but for club bookers and agents too. We did one in Coventry one night in front of an agent's husband, Seamus Walsh. Seamus and his wife Joan have been our friends ever since. It broke our hearts when Seamus died in the Millennium year. He was the first man who genuinely saw something in us, something more than just doing the working men's clubs.

Ian

He apparently went back to his wife and said, 'I have just watched the funniest couple I think I've ever seen.' His wife came to see us the very next night. Joan was also a singer and with her contacts she introduced us to other people and a whole new circle of friends.

Janette

Joan gave us a lot of work for more money than we'd ever earned before. We were up to about £22 a night at this stage in 1969, which was really very good.

Ian

Coventry was also a great stomping ground for us because it was very Scottish. We'd play pubs like The Tam O'Shanter, which was jammed to the rafters with Scots desperate to see their own kind once again.

Janette

The beauty was they didn't want accordions and bagpipes – they just wanted a laugh.

Ian

But on top of that, Joan and Seamus became our closest friends. We'd always stay with them if we were in the area. Seamus had also introduced us both to golf. For the first time since our self-exposed exile from Scotland, Seamus and Joan – along with golf – gave us a life outside of work.

Janette

Also, when we told them we were getting married in October 1969, they were the first to buy us a wedding present.

Ian

But before we got married, we were booked to go back and do the American bases again in Turkey. This time we drove from Frankfurt to Turkey. We got to Bulgaria and had trouble with the Communists yet again. They always seemed to be in the middle of some crisis or another and didn't want to let anyone through their country. They would put ridiculous demands on you like, 'You're not coming through because your hair's too long.' They actually had a barber at the border crossing to cut these poor sods' hair. They said my hair was a disgrace. I wasn't exactly a hippy; we're only talking a bit over my ears. But I went through the rigmarole of having this barber trim my hair. It was just a way of humiliating you. They also would go through every part of your luggage with a fine-tooth comb. They were really messing us about. The guy who was with us, Rick Hardy, was a good schemer. He found a young, smart-looking police officer who looked more intelligent than his colleagues. He then convinced this young officer that, if he ever came to our country, we would not treat him the same way they were treating us now. This obviously struck a chord with the officer. He just snapped his fingers and we were instantly allowed to pack up and move on.

Janette

On the tour of Turkey, with us this time was a Frenchman called Mr Louis who used a real live chimpanzee for his act. Ian was joking at the border that the police were going to cut the chimp's hair too.

When we were driving through Turkey it was boiling hot as usual. We had to stop at this lake one day just to cool down. We let the chimp out of the van and it ran up a tree and wouldn't come back down. Even the ape didn't want to go back in the stinking hot van.

One day on our travels we stopped by a lake. Ian and I went in the water for a swim to cool down. We were the only two people swimming in this lovely lake. But we soon found out why when this huge snake swam past us. The lake was full of water asps. I told Ian, 'Let's get out before we end up like Cleopatra.'

Ian

Even when we got out of the water on to the beach, the sand was alive with scorpions. When we arrived at the US nuclear military base, we told them where we'd been swimming. The soldiers looked horrified and said, 'No one swims in there, man – it's deadly.'

Of course, travelling through Turkey we all got the shits again. Even the chimp had the trots.

Janette

As part of the Frenchman's act he used to dress this chimp
up in a wee sailor's suit. One of the jokes was that he would
give the chimp a plastic potty and it would pretend to have
a shit then empty it over someone in the audience.

Ian

Only this night, the monkey really did have the trots like the
rest of us. So it really did pour shit all over this big GI's head.
The GI's mates were pissing themselves laughing. The whole
place was in fits, but this humiliated GI gets up out of his
chair covered in monkey shit and thumped another soldier
who was laughing at him. Suddenly, all hell broke loose and
it ended up in one huge fist-fight like the Westerns – and all
because this poor chimp had the shits.

Another time after a gig, I was having a break, sitting down
in my kilt when this GI came up and said, 'Are you a real-life
Scotty?'

'Yip – the real thing,' I replied.

Then he asked, 'How many of you are left?'

'Look, it's not like the Red Indians,' I said. 'We weren't
wiped out.'

'Would you like to meet my friend?' he asked. 'He was in
showbusiness too.'

It turned out to be Johnny from the band Johnny and the
Hurricanes; I had all their records, like 'Red River Rock'.
These guys were huge but their careers all stopped like Elvis
the moment they went into the Army.

I then asked these guys where the gents was because I was
bursting for a pee and they pointed me towards some big

doors. However, when I went through the doors all these alarms started going off; it made a terrible din. Suddenly, loads of armed troops instantly appeared, guns at the ready. The sergeant took one look at me and told them that it was OK because I was just one of the acts from the UK. When I asked him where I'd wandered into, he said, 'The place where we keep the heads – we're just 30 miles from the Russians here.' So I had almost stumbled upon nuclear warheads and The Krankies nearly caused an international incident. This was at the height of the Cold War.

When we returned from Turkey to Germany we met up with this dodgy agent who we'll call Ronnie. We were put in touch with him after Janette had met a chap called Bob Johnstone who was in an outfit called The Jumping Jacks – a trampoline act. Bob had given Janette a card and said whenever we wanted to work the American military bases just to give him a call. Janette and I were in Manchester at that time, but there was nothing really on the go, so we gave Bob a call, who in turn put us in touch with Ronnie, who was a black Jewish man from Miami, whom we later found out was actually Mafia. But Ronnie asked us if we wanted to do a tour of Australia, Hong Kong, Kuala Lumpur and Saigon, and we said, 'That sounds great.'

But that night we were having a meal with a Cockney guy we knew and told him about the tour we'd been offered. He basically told us it was a load of rubbish; the place we would really be going was Vietnam. He then handed us that day's newspaper and told me to have a read. It was all about the escalating troubles. We thought this agent wanted us to go to the Far East because we were so damned good, but the truth is he couldn't get anyone else so he thought he'd hire the naïve young Scots. Needless to say, we didn't go.

Janette

In later years, after watching films like *Apocalypse Now*, we actually wished we had gone. I know that sounds strange, but it would have been an incredible experience. Imagine – The Krankies in Vietnam!

Ian

When we told this agent that we didn't want to go, he gave us some more work in Germany at another US base, but he asked us to take a parcel to one of the American sergeants. To this day, we don't know what was in that parcel and, of course, we were idiots for doing it – but we were young and daft. I reckon Ronnie had an illegal gambling ring going on at the bases, like Sergeant Bilko. It had been rife at that time until the Pentagon shut it all down. So I imagine we were carrying money for him in that parcel. Years later, I was speaking to this black American cabaret act, The Clark Brothers, and I told them about our experience with this parcel. They told me that Ronnie was famous for using the cabaret acts to launder his money. It's a good one for the CV though, isn't it – money smuggler.

3

THE KRANKIES...
'TIL DEATH US DO PART

Janette

After Germany, we returned home and got married, with the wedding at the Burnbrae Hotel in Bearsden. My mum and dad couldn't really afford it, but dad was determined to pay. We had about 110 guests for a beautiful sit-down meal and, in 1969, it cost Dad around £2,500, so he really pushed the boat out for us.

Ian

That wedding really did wipe Janette's dad out, but he didn't give a damn because it was for his little girl. We spent our wedding night at Janette's parents' house and I'll never forget how naïve her mother was. I was sitting there watching the telly and Janette was packing up all the wedding presents to take back to our council house we'd just got in Peterlee in County Durham, and her old dear said to me, 'When your father and I were married, we couldn't wait to get up to the bedroom, but you two are sitting here watching the telly.'

To give her dad credit, he leaned over and said, 'Mary, they've been together for three-and-a-half years.'

A bit shocked, she said, 'Oh my God, I never even thought of that.' She had come from much more innocent times.

Janette

The next day, we drove to Peterlee and even did a gig that night. By that time we were working the north-east every night as it was booming with clubs. Scotland was still in the dark ages at that point as the strict licensing laws wouldn't let anything open. The pubs still shut at 10.00pm sharp.

Ian

Of course, because we'd been together for a few years and were married, it's only natural that our families started asking if we were going to have children. The honest truth is we never really thought about it. We never tried to have kids or tried not to have kids. We just got on with working.

Janette

We've never planned anything out in our life, never once said, 'Right, it's time we started playing these types of clubs or time to have children.' Ian and I simply aren't like that. The only thing we did plan at the time was trading in our Morris Oxford when we got married for a left-hand drive Mercedes because Ian had always wanted a Merc.

Ian

The bloody thing turned out to have been a Portuguese taxi.

It was a heap of shite. It blew up on the motorway shortly after I bought the bugger.

Janette

By this point we had a manager, Bob Deplidge, who managed the company Beverley Artists. He was booking 600 clubs at that time with huge acts like Roy Orbinson and Gene Pitney. Even in those days, these big names worked both the social clubs and the nightclubs.

Bob also told us that he couldn't sell Jinty and Tough, which was what we'd been going out on the circuit as, and told us we needed something else. Well, I'd been The Krankie Kids when I went to Manchester the first time with Margaret, so we just dropped the 'Kids' and became, plain and simply, The Krankies. If we'd known what we were doing to ourselves, maybe we'd have thought longer about it. There are friends of ours in the business even today who call us Ian and Janette Krankie. Many journalists reported it as fact that Krankie was our surname. So to say that the name stuck is an understatement.

The following year in 1970, Bob sent us down to London for an audition for a summer season in Blackpool. We'd played in London before at Douglas House, which was the headquarters for the American Forces.

Ian

Unfortunately, when we got there for the audition we immediately realised that the people we'd been sent to meet were gangsters, the white suit, black tie brigade. We actually got the season in Blackpool on the South Pier that summer. Topping the bill were Freddie and the Dreamers and we were bottom. The 'From Scotland' bit on the poster was in a bigger typeface than our name. We earned £50 a week, which was a cut in money because we were earning a lot more at the clubs by that point.

Janette

We opened our act with the Frank and Nancy Sinatra song 'Something Stupid'. The curtains would open and I was standing at the same height as Ian on a platform with a long black-and-white dress, then halfway through the song I used to step down and leave the dress standing.

Ian

The impact was instantaneous … it'd bring the house down.

Janette

We were in digs in Waterloo Road in Blackpool and instantly fell in love with the place as the buzz was incredible. We were always being invited to mayors' functions and civic receptions, and the people really looked after us.

Ian

We were the youngsters so the other more established acts would take us under their wing – Tommy Steele, Mary Hopkins, Freddie Starr, Joseph Locke and Hilda Baker. These were names that we'd only heard of and they would come up to us and say, 'Are you going to the party at the Lemon Tree tonight?' and we'd be like, 'We canny really afford it.' Every one of them would tell us, 'Nonsense, you're coming.' They would pay for all our food and drinks, everything, because we were bottom of the bill and they'd all been there at some point in their lives.

Janette

Freddie Garretty, who had number-one hits at the time, used to take us to his beautiful big house in Manchester on a Sunday for dinner with his family. Ian and Freddie were about the same size so he used to give Ian all his old shirts and suits.

Ian

I had never seen a lifestyle like it. His garden had fountains and a swimming pool. I thought, 'I want a bit of this.' Don't get me wrong though, they wouldn't be like that with everyone, because pros are pretty funny that way. They'll only take to you if they see talent in you and like you as a person. But once they see that, they let you into their inner sanctum.

Janette

Freddie Starr was always offering to take me out to football matches. I used to be terrified of him because he drove his sports car so fast. He never tried anything on with me, I think he just liked me. But he has those really scary eyes and always called me 'Jan', and Ian was shortened to 'Ee'. Only a Scouser could find a way of shortening the name Ian.

By this time, we had a bit of money and Ian thought it'd be fun to buy a dinghy. We bought a 12ft boat with a wee Mercury outboard. We didn't have anywhere to lock it up so we used to chain the engine to the end of our bed in the guesthouse. These musicians who were staying with us used to come in and say 'Bloody hell – what do you two get up to at night?'

Years later, we'd bump into the same guys and they'd still be going on about that outboard strapped to our bed.

Ian

That started our love affair with boats that would continue over 30 years until the present. We now have a 36ft Grandbanks motor cruiser.

Janette

But back then we used to take our wee dinghy up and down the river and potter about in it. It was a great way of spending your spare time in the afternoon. Life was definitely a lot of fun.

4

THE BIG TIME FOR WEE JIMMY

Janette

We saw Jimmy Clitheroe in Scarborough the year before our first summer season in 1970. He was a little man who played a little boy. He used to have his own radio show called *The Clitheroe Kid* and had been a massive star, who had been discovered by George Formby and appeared in his movies. It was Clitheroe we used to listen to when we were kids, but we never thought of doing an act in the same way.

Ian

An old comic, Freddie Seles, watched our act from the side of the stage and afterwards he asked us, 'Can you take constructive criticism?'

'Sure,' I said, because we were always up for learning, especially from the old pros.

He then told us, 'You've got it all wrong.'

This was a bit of a surprise because this particular night we thought we'd done really well. He then told me that I would never ever be a comic as long as I'm standing beside Janette because, 'with all due respect, the funny person is not you – you tell a gag, but I can get you a hundred people who tell gags – she's the funny one.'

Janette

Freddie then turned to me and said, 'You're small ... why don't you use your height more?' He then told me to find a character for my height. His suggestion was for me to dress up as a St Trinian schoolgirl, but I thought that may be a bit tacky. But we knew what he meant – he just wanted us to change our whole act round.

Ian

Freddie wanted me to be the straight man. This was the complete opposite of everything we'd ever done. Up until then, I was doing the funny lines and Janette was the clown.

Janette

We went back to Scotland before being booked for Barrow and Furness Labour Club and only had two 20-minute segments to do on the night. One was visual comedy and one was doing our Scottish stuff – dancing and what have you. This club said they'd give us £22 but they needed three slots. So we racked our brains about what we were going to do. Back at Ian's home in Clydebank, we went up into the loft where we found his grandfather's boots, his little brother Colin's red school cap and blazer and his older brother Alistair's khaki shorts. It looked great as the boots were far too big for me and the blazer was too small and tight like

Norman Wisdom. I still wear his grandfather Robert's boots to this day. So we went way back down to Barrow and Furness with a few school gags but still not much of a clue about what we were going to do.

To open the act, Ian came out and said he'd sing a song. Just as he'd started, I walked through the audience dressed as Jimmy and said, 'Excuse me, what ye doin' up there, mister – are you a group?' This woman said to me in the audience, 'Eee, sonny, have you lost yer mam?' From the first moment I did the act, people thought I really was a wee boy.

Ian

I knew from that moment we'd found a winner as the place erupted in fits of laughter. I remember afterwards saying to Janette, 'I think this is better than anything we've ever done before.' That was just before our summer season in Blackpool in 1970. But we didn't take Jimmy to Blackpool with us because it was our first summer season and also because we thought the audience would be too sophisticated for that sort of act – stupid, eh?

Janette

We were also a bit apprehensive because Jimmy Clitheroe was still on the go at the time and we didn't want to be seen as nicking his schoolboy act, even though it was very different as it was a woman dressing up as a wee boy.

Ian

With all the dodgy folk we used to meet and work with I was surprised we didn't get into a really major incident sooner because we played some really tough venues. One of them was the Downhill in Sunderland – the toughest club in the north-east of England, where they used to do strip shows on a Sunday morning. Some folk have no respect for the Sabbath!

Our comic friend Johnny Hammond told us of an incident he had been involved in when he arrived for his gig and loads of police were outside The Downhill. He was met at the door by a stripper who was in hysterics. The police then explained to him, 'Look, we've got a problem … there's a man sitting inside with a gun on his table and we don't think he's mentally stable. What we'd like you to do is go out there and do your normal act and, when you distract him, we'll grab him.'

This honestly was the hardest club to win over in England. It was notorious for it. If you got past 12 minutes, you were lucky. It was full of shipbuilders from Sunderland. They used to read their newspapers when you were on.

So Johnny went out there and he was dying on his backside. As usual, no one was laughing, except the lunatic with the gun on his table. Two policemen in boilersuits asked the gunman if they could sit beside him and, before he could answer, they grabbed him and marched him out.

Johnny was still on stage at that point and he shouted after them, 'When you've finished with him, you can come back for the rest of these bastards.'

We were playing a similar place called Comrades Social Club, or 'Anti-social' as we renamed it. There was a strongman on the bill with us called Brutus. So we went on and we were only getting a smattering of applause, no laughter at all. Afterwards, it was the turn of Brutus and he got nothing either. He started tearing a telephone directory and they were all shouting, 'Piss off … we can all do that.' He came off stage and the booker came up to us all and said, 'Well, you can clear off because you're shite and you're not getting any money.' The strongman said, 'You booked me – you pay me.' The booker started giving Brutus more verbal until the strongman picked him up with one hand and hung him on a coat-hook on the back of the dressing-room door. Brutus then got the booker's wallet out his jacket, took £12 and buggered off.

We were pissing ourselves laughing but we eventually helped this irate booker down off the peg and he asked us to go on again since Brutus had left by this point. By the time we'd finished our third act, the booker was absolutely steaming and he said to us, 'Well, if you think you're getting paid for that load of shite you can bugger off too.' He owed us £18 and one thing led to another … basically, I swung for him with a mic stand.

The next minute, this huge miner appeared covered from head to toe in tattoos that are all spelt wrong and he chucked us out.

Outside, I was sitting in our new Zodiac car when I saw this pished booker staggering about the street – I ended up chasing him around the car park in my car.

But I still didn't get my money. They were awful clubs to play in Sunderland … but they were great training.

Then on Christmas Eve we went to Millview in Sunderland and again the booker wouldn't give us the money because he needed it himself to buy presents. This guy was a big ex-policeman and he threatened to chuck me out on my arse. So Janette said, 'Let's go.' The next day, I returned to try and get my money while Janette was sitting outside in the car. Suddenly she saw me running up Sunderland beachfront being chased by this huge bloody ex-cop. We were really depressed because we hadn't got our money and were skint for Christmas.

Janette

A year later, they actually booked us again. By this point, we had built up a good following and were actually becoming a bit of a name on the scene. But there was no way I was going back to this club after the appalling way they'd treated us, but told them we'd do it. I said to Ian, 'I'm going to make them sweat.' So I waited to 7.30 when the club was full and I phoned this big idiot and said, 'It's Janette Krankie here.'

'Oh, hello, bonny lass, are you lost?' he said cheerfully.

'Oh no,' I said, 'we know exactly where your club is and, frankly, you can shove it up your arse.'

This left him right in the thick of it. The crowd was getting restless by this point and we heard later he went on to the stage and said, 'The little Krankie is no' coming – because she told me to stuff my club up my arse.' It cost him a fortune having to pay everyone back. Revenge is definitely a dish best served cold.

Because we were gigging so much, we got to meet a lot of fellow performers. In 1971, we did a season at the Derbyshire Miner's Holiday Club and were on the bill with a comedian called Joe Black who was an old theatre comic. We were supposed to be doing sketches with him, but it wasn't our humour at all. He was doing send-ups of Romeo and Juliet and we were what I suppose you'd call 'alternative' back then, doing songs from the charts and what have you.

On that same bill was a double act called The Garland Sisters with a girl called Cheryl who eventually married Roger De Courcey. This was the first time we ever met Roger and Ian went for a round of golf with him. At this time, Roger hadn't 'met' Nookie Bear or found national TV fame but had, in fact, been a very good singer in London's West End.

Ian

I get on with most folk but I didn't like Roger at all when I first met him. He was a typical bolshy Londoner. After that round of golf, I came back home in a filthy mood and said to Janette, 'That man's not right for Cheryl. He was so rude to everyone on the golf course – including me – I felt like walking away.'

Janette

We later did a summer season with Roger De Courcey and Duncan Norvelle at Bournemouth. Roger and Duncan didn't get on very well, as Roger would be moaning at everyone – including us. He said there were too many children in the audience because of us and it made it harder for him to control. He was basically having a tough time of it on stage, really struggling. One night after a particularly poor performance, I was walking down a corridor backstage when I saw Roger getting hold of his puppet Nookie Bear. He booted the bear as hard as he could against a wall, then said to this crumpled heap of a puppet, 'You'd think one of us could get a bloody laugh out there.'

About ten minutes later, when he'd calmed down a bit, Roger knocked on my dressing-room door and asked if he could borrow some eyeliner. I asked why and he showed me Nookie, with his nose all scraped – he needed my eyeliner to colour in his nose before going back on stage.

Duncan Norvelle had just bought a brand-new customised car, a Cosgrove Sierra, when they'd just come out. Duncan wanted to park it right outside his dressing-room window so he could keep an eye on it. So he got a letter from the company manager warning him not to park it there as it was blocking the exit, but he still wouldn't move it. He then got a letter from the theatre manager again asking him to shift the car and, eventually, the promoter wrote too – but he *still* refused to move it.

It was causing a right fuss so, eventually, Roger took Duncan aside and said, 'Look, Duncan, I used to be a bit like you, very headstrong and bombastic, but it got me nowhere.'

Duncan replied, 'Yes, but the difference between you and I Roger is that I've got talent.'

Roger went ballistic and chased him out the theatre. They hated each other after that and no wonder.

The crunch came one night, though, when Duncan missed his call to go on stage, which meant Roger had to go on first, even though he was above Duncan on the bill, then Norvelle came on afterwards, which is simply not done. By rights – according to theatre etiquette – Duncan shouldn't have come on stage at all that night.

At the finale, we all stepped forward with the whole cast, took our bow and, as the curtain went down, Roger punched Duncan right in the face, but they both had to quickly compose themselves as the curtain went straight back up again for the encore – it was like a comedy in itself.

Top left: Janette on holiday – with skirt tucked into knickers. *Top right*: Sitting on a stuffed tiger on the Isle of Man.

Above left: Ian with horse and (*above right*) with something a bit nippier – standing proudly beside his first car.

Top: Janette at her cousin's wedding with her father, mother, granny and grandpa.

Above: Janette's parents in 1990, a year before her mother died.

Us as budding performers.

Top right: Ian at the Clydebank rep Theatre in 1964, with a young Barbara Rafferty, who went on to find fame as Ella from Rab C Nesbitt. *Top left* and *above*: Janette with her pal Margeret Murray in 1965 as The Krankie Kids.

Top: Our first publicity photo in 1966.

Above: The Tough family at our wedding in 1969. *Left to right*: Ian's big brother Alastair, dad Alex, mum Betty, Ian and his wee brother Clin. *Opposite*: Janette in her wedding dress and (*inset*) the happy couple.

KRANKIES

All enquiries
to
BOB DEPLIDGE

A taste of things to come! Our first contact card in 1969.

Top: On our way. Janette as 'wee Jimmy Krankie' in 1971.

Above: Getting recognition as we win Club Act of the Year 1978. It would be nearly a quarter of a century before a Krankie was nominated for an award again.

Top: With 'fellow' ventriloquist John Bouchier.

Above: Ian demonstrations his unconventional 'voice throwing' techniques.

Ian

Surprisingly over the years, I got to like Roger a lot when I realised all his brashness was just a front and we are good friends to this day.

Janette

When we did Derbyshire Miner's Club in 1971, it was a 20-week-long season. It was really hard work because the first eight weeks of the season we entertained the mentally and physically handicapped, many of whom would sit in the front row in their basket chairs.

I used to come through the audience as Jimmy, but the carers would tell me not to go near any of the audience who were wearing green badges because they were really dangerous and likely to lash out. They would even give some of them injections to calm them down before we went on.

One night, when I was walking down the aisle shouting, 'Has anyone seen me mam?' this big female carer grabbed me by the arm and got her big syringe out ready to give me an injection. She honestly thought I was one of the handicapped kids who was causing a scene. I was shouting, 'I'm in the show, I'm in the show, don't give me a jab.'

In the October of that year, our agent at the time, Billy Forest, sent us for a month of gigs in Jersey for the first time. Down there we worked for a man called Jimmy Muir who was from Partick in Glasgow and owned The Sunshine Hotel.

Paul Daniels had been there for the whole summer. I'd never come across him before but knew of him. He'd been supporting an Irish comic, Bal Mone, but when we arrived Bal had left so we were now top of the bill for the first time

– something I think Paul resented. Paul was a super act but, personally, he was such a bore.

We were all living in the same hotel and he'd have a trick in every pocket. We'd be sitting in the bar having a conversation with some guest or one of the other acts and he'd butt in doing some bloody card trick.

After a month, we were sick and tired of him and our patience had just about run out. One night, he came over to our table and butted into our conversation as usual – that's when Ian told him to piss off.

Ian

I was so annoyed after a month of being constantly pestered by him that something just snapped and I swung for him. I didn't hit him that badly, but he still went flying off the bar stool on to his arse. I had simply cracked. But, amazingly, a punch in the gob had no effect whatsoever on Paul.

I would actually play golf with him after that incident and he was still the same pesky wee man, doing tricks at every turn as if nothing had happened. But to give the man credit, at the end of that run he bought Janette and I going-away presents. So I take my hat off to him; he might have been a pain but he was also a gentleman.

Janette

One of my good friends is a singer/dancer who had been seriously injured in a car accident after she'd fallen asleep at the wheel. She was in hospital when Paul Daniels sent her flowers – this was years before he met Debbie McGee. The roses had a note asking her out on a date when she was fit. So when she went out for a meal with Paul for the first time, he said to her over dinner, 'Will you marry me?' It was their first date. She said, 'Paul, I don't know you at all,' so he offered to take her to America for three weeks' holiday, no strings attached, but just so she had an opportunity to get to know him and decide if she wanted to get married. My friend thought three weeks in America would also be a good recovery period for her after the accident and so off they went.

When she came back, I asked her how she'd got on. She said, 'Oh, Janette, it was awful. Every morning I got up and we'd go down for breakfast and he'd have tricks out of every pocket for me and the other guests. I was that sick of him making my boiled egg disappear every morning that I'd order a fried one.'

She then told me that she got so pissed off with him she couldn't even last the whole holiday. Instead, she just slipped a note under his door saying, 'Paul, you really are an amazing magician – you can even make your women disappear.'

Ian

I'm actually in a society called The Water Rats with Paul. There's only 200 of us in the world and you have to wait until someone dies to get in.

The King Rats include people like Paul, Danny La Rue and the late entertainers Bob Hope and Les Dawson. It's an organisation of charitable entertainers and you can only become a member if you're asked to join, but our work is never publicised.

Janette

We were booked to go back to Jersey in the spring of 1972.

In the Christmas of 1971, though, we played at the British Forces bases around Europe with two dancers from The Sunshine Hotel. It was called *Have a Krankie Kristmas*. We toured all over with a Jewish agent, Mickey Hayes, and his wife. Mickey had a terrible toupée and an old Mercedes that he drove us around in. Mickey said he suffered from asthma and we couldn't get him to put the heating on in that bloody car for love nor money. So there we were, driving through Germany in the middle of winter, frozen solid in the back seat of his beloved Merc.

Ian

We also had a singing and dancing act with us and Mickey would only stop at expensive motorway filling stations for food, so none of the acts could afford to eat. We were all starving – and freezing.

It got so cold one day that we decided to make a fire in the back of this old Mercedes. I got a fag packet and lit it and we were all warming our hands on it when Mickey says to his wife, 'Mary, do you smell burning?'

'Yes, dear,' she replied.

I said, 'Don't worry yer arse, Mickey, it's just a wee fire we've got going in the back here.'

Well, he slammed on his brakes and threatened to chuck us all out on the Autobahn. Despite our protests, the bugger still never turned on that bloody heater.

Janette

The digs we had on that tour in Germany were old nursing homes for some reason. We actually spent Christmas in one of those places, but we did what we could to make this draughty old place look festive, cutting down a tree in the garden and decorating it the best we could.

We were in Hamlin one day on tour in the early part of 1972, and I went shopping as usual. Before I went off, Ian said to me, 'Now, Janette, whatever you do, if you see a man with a flute don't follow him.'

We returned from Germany and immediately went off to Ireland as we had a load of gigs. We got there the day before Bloody Sunday in Northern Ireland and were staying in the Tudor Rooms Hotel in Dublin where the staff were so nice to us – but that all changed after the news started filtering through the next day. We were supposed to be flying out of Ireland that Sunday, but because of the trouble they closed Dublin Airport and we had to go back to the hotel. As soon as we walked back in, they were shouting at us, 'It all your fault – it's the Scottish Protestants who should have been shot,' and that was just the staff, the very ones who'd been so nice to us the night before. The atmosphere was very strained and we were frightened.

Ian

One guest told us quite chillingly that we shouldn't step outside the hotel as we'd get lynched. At that very moment in Dublin, they were trying to set fire to the British Embassy. Anything British – cars and what have you – was being trashed and burned, but we couldn't get out. So we had to get the boat from Dun Laoghaire to Holyhead. On our way there, they were burning Union Jacks in the streets.

Janette

We had never been so happy to leave a place in all our lives. We were in a force-nine gale during that ferry crossing and we felt awful, with everyone throwing up, but we were just glad to get away.

5

THE YANKEES MEET THE KRANKIES

Janette

In 1972, we decided not to do a summer season and concentrated on the big clubs where we'd be on the same bill as Roy Orbinson, Neil Sedaka, Gene Pitney, Frankie Lane – albeit we were doing the coffee slot in between their sets.

Ian

The Americans were the nicest top-of-the-bill acts we'd ever met, except for The Everly Brothers, who seemed to me to be a bit out of their faces. It was so sad to see them struggle. In a funny way, it did us the world of good because we stole the show that night in front of a huge audience. They were all there to see The Everly Brothers. I had bought everything they'd ever done and was a huge fan, but they were horrendous. They were so bad they even fell out with each other. It was such a shame. But when we'd come back on, we got rapturous applause.

Janette

After that gig, we started to climb up the bills. These cabaret clubs were huge. There was the Manchester Golden Garter, Jollies in Stoke-on-Trent, Talk of the North … loads and loads of these fantastic clubs, where over 1,500 people would go for a meal in beautiful surroundings and dance to an eight-piece band – real class and I loved them.

Ian

It was a great shame when these fabulous venues died away. I think, ultimately, the big American names killed them off. I remember Satchmo came over and charged £25,000 for one week's work from Batley Variety. Wakefield Variety up the road were like, 'Right, we'll beat that,' and paid Shirley Bassey £30,000. It's almost exactly the same situation many football clubs are in now, where they haven't realised that they can't actually pay this money.

Later on, they were turning more to acts like us, whom they could pay £2,000 for a week and still get 700 punters in.

Janette

We started off on £500 a week, doing seven days a week in these clubs until we introduced the girl dancers, then we became more like a big cabaret act. But I loved those days, they were just such great venues.

Ian

Those were the best times. It was pure class and I'd love to be doing something like that again. The only place they had something like that in Scotland was the Piccadilly in

Glasgow's Sauchiehall Street, which is now Victoria's nightclub. But down south the place was full of them. We were rubbing shoulders with the greats in these places like Tommy Cooper. It was a great shop window.

Janette

We got drunk with Tommy in his dressing room one time. He'd never leave his room when he wasn't on stage and he wouldn't let you go until you'd help him finish a bottle – or three.

Ian

I'll never forget the time at Bailey's in Leicester where we worked with Tommy for a week and he said to us to both on the first night, 'What do you drink?' Janette said, 'Whisky,' and I said, 'Dry Martini.' When we went to his dressing room after the show, he had a bottle of each for us. It was a nightmare because he wanted you to stay until the last drop. The thing is, he'd be in that dressing room until about 4.00am, long after the show, then he'd go home, have a meal, walk about and not go to bed until seven at night, get up, have his breakfast and do a gig. He completely turned his day upside down. He was nuts but great fun and a lovely big man.

Janette

Neil Sedaka was very nice to us too. We worked with him at the Wooky Hollow in Liverpool when he was going through a stage of not being quite as big as he was in his heyday. I remember he went berserk one day when he gave his band his musical arrangements and they spilled beer all over them; he hated unprofessionalism like that.

Neil was in Liverpool with his daughter who was ten at the time and sang some of the act with him.

Ian

I remember his wee girl coming into our dressing room and she told you everything. I'd be like, 'How are you?' and she'd say in her little American accent, 'Oh, Mummy and Daddy have had a row today.' And nosy me would be like, 'Wow, what were they rowing about?' But I was caught out when Neil shouted from outside our dressing room, 'Honey, come out of there and stop annoying people.'

But the nicest of them all was Gene Pitney. He came up to us in the Cresta, Solihull, and said, 'You're very funny. You two will become stars and I'll remind you both I told you that the next time I see you.'

Janette

I asked if I could buy an album from him and he gave it to us for nothing, then signed it

'Until the day you are stars. It was a pleasure to work with such a fantastic talent.'

Ian

We met him about ten years later while we were doing *Blankety Blank* with him and he came straight up to us and said, 'What did I tell you guys?' So it was lovely that such a big name showed so much faith in us.

Janette

Those were great days performing at these magnificent clubs. You'd drive up to the venues thinking, 'I wonder who we'll be on with tonight?' We'd arrive and a name like Frankie Lane would be up in lights and we'd both shout, 'Yer beauty!'

At around that time in the early 1970s, there were occasions when we weren't just sharing the bill with the greats – we'd find that we were sharing our digs with them too, along with other 'unconventional' guests. We were in Leeds doing Batley Variety Club and staying in digs run by a posh Jewish lady. Engelbert Humperdinck used to stay at the same digs. She adored Engelbert and even named her dog after him. The way she ran her guesthouse was the lower down the bill you were, the lower your bedroom was in the guesthouse. So when we started out we were literally sleeping in the basement; by the time we topped the bill at the Berkley, we were 'honoured' – so she told us – to be given Engelbert's room.

Ian

Yes, but you could have knocked us down with a feather when we found out that this posh guesthouse doubled as a brothel. It was guesthouse by night when all the performers were in after the shows, and a brothel by day. This woman would never let you answer her phone or go out in the back garden where she had a huge shed. But there was a Welsh comic, Dave Swan, staying there too, and when we came back from a gig one night, he was like, 'Let's have a look in that shed.' So we sneaked down and found the key and opened it up. Sure enough, it was a fetish room with chains and belts and a harness hanging from the roof. Dave started roaring with laughter and woke up the entire neighbourhood. Every light in the house was going on and we had to rush back to our room before the landlady caught us. But she was obviously a high-class hooker. You could just imagine her catering to the fetishes of Chiefs of Police and High Court judges, which is the only type of clientele she would have relished, being an inverted snob.

Janette

When Ian and Dave discovered what was in that shed, everything started to make sense. For example, it was the only guesthouse I've ever been in anywhere in the world where they changed your sheets every day. It suddenly dawned on us that our beds were obviously in use during the evenings when we were out at work.

But Wales also had some very strange digs for the entertainers. We stayed with Mrs Jones in Cardiff who told us, 'I only have top-of-the-bills staying here – never chorus line or musicians.' She then went on to give us the house rules, which were

'There are two toilets in this house, one upstairs and one downstairs – but don't use the upstairs one for solids.'

Ian

I asked her why she didn't like musicians and she said she'd once had a nasty experience with them. She explained, 'These two boys turned up at the door from the new theatre and were lovely looking lads, but I said I only had one room left but they didn't mind sharing. So they went to their room and I thought I'd ask if they'd like a cup of tea and a slice of toast, but when I walked in I found them

lying on the bed naked. Well, I knew right away, you see –
drugs.' We were both killing ourselves laughing.

Janette

In 1973, we were working with an act called Mickey and
Gerry. Mickey was a beautiful French singer and Gerry was a
Belgian trombone player, who adored me for some reason.
He'd always be saying, 'Aw, my little Janette, you're so lovely.'

Ian

I absolutely adored Jersey. It was such a different and relaxing
place to live. I'd never seen things like people surfing before,
wonderful restaurants, clean sea and warm air. A gorgeous
place. The hotel owner Jimmy Muir would take us out to the
best restaurants and got us into fine wines. That's where we
really got a taste for good living.

Janette

That was the first time I'd tried an oyster with champagne.
Big Jimmy Muir – who owned The Sunshine Hotel – would
take us out every Sunday. Because we did such a long season
for him over many years this was the first time we had to
start producing our own shows. You couldn't just do your act
as you had to find numbers for the dancers and that's when
I started directing for the first time, with all my dance-school
experience coming in very handy.

Ian

I'd be thinking up and writing sketches, so when a new film
like *Star Wars* came out in 1977, we'd do that immediately.

Janette

I'd do R2-D2 or Bugsie Malone. It was wonderful training because every year we went back we had to have new shows.

In 1974, though, we didn't go back to Jersey for the summer as we did a season for Fred Pontin at Pontin's Holiday Camp in Torquay where we shared a rented house with a comic called Alan Fox. One morning, we had a phone call from the police asking to speak to Tommy Duffy, which was Alan's real name. His son had been knocked down and killed on his way to school and we had to go and tell Alan. He came back with his family and it was awful for them. We spent the whole summer with this poor family in mourning. His wife was wailing all the time. They had a nine-year-old daughter and we used to take her out, just to get her away from it all.

Ian

That was a sad, sad time. I saw Alan have an audience in convulsions with tears running down his face. It was tragic. He was making people laugh while he was breaking his heart. I don't know how he could do that.

6

TV ON THE CV

Ian

In 1974, we did our first ever TV appearance on the Saturday night show *The Wheel Tappers and Shunters Social Club*, based in a working men's club. We did the ventriloquist dummy act, where I'd have Janette on my knee and throw her around.

In those days the club acts weren't really recognised as television material, as TV was still dominated by comics like Frankie Howerd and Jimmy Edwards. TV didn't want us because they thought of us as being a bit cheap and vulgar, and not for the viewing masses – there was mass snobbery in the TV world back then.

But the head of light entertainment at Granada Televsion was Johnny Hamp who'd just proved them all wrong by having a huge success with a show called *The Comedians*, which was full of young, new comedians back in the 1970s. So he had devised this new show *The Wheel Tappers And*

Shunters Social Club that would bring the club acts to prime-time television.

The funny thing was at the time we thought we were playing to the mass of the British public in the clubs, but of course the real masses were sitting at home watching TV. As soon as we got on that show for the first time we realised how wrong we were. Suddenly people would recognise us in the streets, our money for gigs also suddenly went from £18 a night to hundreds of pounds a night. So TV meant recognition and money to us.

But it was nerve wracking going into this completely new environment. The producers would stop you in the middle of your act to move a camera then get you to do the same punchline in front of the same audience again. It was so alien. But I realised quickly we also had to strike within three minutes as we didn't have the luxury of being able to say, 'Oh well, we're on for an hour anyway,' where you have time to build up the crowd.

For that TV appearance, *The Daily Record* – which was, at the time, the biggest national newspaper in Scotland – did a double-page spread on us. That was our first big interview. That day, I was back in Glasgow and I popped into Lauder's pub and bumped into the famous Scots comic Chick Murray, who inspired people like Billy Connolly to go into stand-up. I got chatting with Chick and he said, 'Are you busy?'

'Not really,' I said.

'Come with me,' he said. Chick had such a legendary dry sense of humour. We were walking through George Square when this guy was running past us with 20 parcels precariously balanced and Chick said, 'Excuse me, do you have a light?' Well, this guy put all these parcels down and got his matches out of his pocket, when Chick then said, 'You know, I think I should give up smoking,' and just walked away. That was just Chick. He was like that all the time. He then spotted an American couple trying to take a picture of a monument so he went and stood right in front of their camera.

After he'd finished fooling around, we went into the Horseshoe Bar for a drink. I said, 'What are you having, Chick?' knowing full well getting a drink out of him was like getting blood from a stone. He just put his hand on my shoulder and said, 'Don't be stupid, you don't buy a drink in here today.'

'Why?' I asked.

'How many times have you been on the middle pages in the *Daily Record* on the day you're about to be seen on television?'

'Never.'

'Exactly,' he said, tapping the side of his nose. 'Within three minutes, every bastard in this bar will be queuing up to buy you drinks – and me as well.' And he was right. I ended up having a great afternoon with him on the piss.

By the time we returned to Jersey in 1975, we were packing out The Sunshine Hotel. I don't think we really knew what we were worth. We were just glad to be playing to a full house every night.

Janette

We were still young and naïve, but Jimmy Muir would always be keen for us to come back the next year and would say to me, 'Make sure you keep taking the Smarties [my contraceptive pill], Janette, as I don't want you getting pregnant.'

But the truth is, we were also in love with Jersey and loved coming back. That summer of 1975, we also bought a bigger boat and, after Sunday lunch, we used to go out and have a bit of sex at sea – those were the days.

Ian

We were having a very passionate afternoon one day in the boat, when I looked up and suddenly I could see the French coast. I was shitting myself in case I didn't have enough fuel to get us back.

But we used to have it off everywhere in Jersey. There wasn't a place Janette and I hadn't 'christened' from the golf course to the high street. It was amazing we never got caught.

That year, we also met the comic Dustin Gee, who had the same management company as us. Dustin was great but he was very off the wall. To me, he was ground-breaking, doing things I'd never seen or heard before. He would be doing incredible impressions of David Bowie and Doctor Who. He would walk on stage to 'The Teddy Bears' Picnic' because he was a camp act. I'd never seen anyone try to carry off a camp act in a working men's club and I was sure he'd be eaten alive – but he had the boldness to carry it. He was one of the first of his kind.

Janette

We lived in Jimmy Muir's cottage and Dustin was in the high flats across from the hotel. We used to go to this beautiful beach every day with Dustin and his boyfriend, who was a bit mentally unstable.

Ian

There was a café at the top of this beach, which had stairs linking it to the water's edge. Dustin would say to the café owners, 'Would you like me to go down and sell ice lollies for you?' So he'd get the tray around his neck and walk around the beach – but with a difference, because he was completely stark naked. He had the tray covering his willy. It was only after people had bought their ice cream and he was walking away that they would realise he was naked.

Sometimes, one of our musicians, The Vicar – because his father was a vicar, of course – would come out with us. He'd wear a vicar's collar and walk into the Pontin's camp while they were playing bingo. Bold as you like, he'd go up on to the stage and say into the microphone, 'Yes, my son, I think this is the place for you …' – that was my queue to run on stage with a raincoat, flash all the old dears, then we'd run outside, jump in the car and race away.

You could just imagine all these old dears afterwards going, 'Was that the half-time entertainment?' But I was always flashing people. In fact, you could say that I was a serial flasher.

One night, Dustin asked if Janette and I would come along with him to judge a beauty pageant. I really didn't want to go because I hate these beauty contests as you take your life in your hands if you pick the wrong ones. Dustin always took his dog Sinbad with him. But he was always smoking joints so we'd get into his car full of smoke and even his dog was high.

Janette

Dustin then picks the ugliest girl as the winner. She really was a bit rough, but he made her feel great by saying she looked like Anne Margaret.

Ian

I swear the one he picked had a limp, squint eyes and missing teeth. But Dustin held her hand up and said 'my winner'. The place erupted in fury; they were throwing ashtrays at us, calling us all the names under the sun – we had to make a sharp exit.

But, sadly, the following season Dustin's boyfriend committed suicide by throwing himself off the high flats in Jersey.

Dustin himself died of a heart attack in 1986 after suffering from cardiomyopathy. He'd had a heart condition all his life but had never told anyone. His mother told me at his funeral that he'd been born with an enlarged heart. It basically gave up because he had been using drugs, poppers or whatever they were. I felt he was a very frustrated guy. He got his big break when he did the *Les Dennis and Dustin Gee* show. That was an excellent show and he could mimic people like Robert Mitchum to a tee.

Janette

Dustin came and stayed with us once when we were living in Coventry. He was desperate to watch Princess Anne's wedding on our first colour television – he loved our new telly. We just sat there for hours with him and he was wonderful company. He's a great loss.

We did a season on the Isle of Man during the blistering

hot summer of 1976, where we meet The Grumbleweeds. We took the boat with us too, on the trailer. The show opened on my birthday on 16 May at The Palace Hotel, which also had a huge casino. The Grumbleweeds were at The Lido, which was also part of the casino. We were in one show and they were in the other.

We were living in a place called Peel with our musical director Davie Squires. In the afternoon, Davie would come out fishing with us. One day, we were about two miles from the coast and I'm topless sunbathing up the front of the boat when at the back Davie shouts, 'I've caught a big one here.' It was a beautiful 15lb cod and we went back and cooked it up – it was delicious.

So the next day, we thought we'd go back to the same spot and Davie caught another fish, but it was a massive conger eel. He reeled it in and I swear it was about 5ft long with a head the thickness of a man's leg.

Ian shouted, 'Davie, cut the line, I can't afford to have this eel in the boat ...' But as they've gone to get the clippers, this giant eels whipped itself up into the boat. They jumped backwards and I tipped off the front, topless, into the water. By now, the boat's unstable with the weight of Davie and Ian at the back with the engine, so it was listing badly and started filling with water.

Davie made the quickest decision of his life when he said, 'I'll swim for help,' even though we were two miles from shore – and that meant swimming through jelly fish the size of dustbin lids. So Davie headed off to shore. It was terrifying as every time we tried to rest on the hull, it would sink below the surface. The bow would only come up about eight inches above the water for about ten seconds which would give you a rest, then you had to swim away and wait for it hopefully to come back up again. So I told Ian to dive down and get a lifejacket for himself.

Ian

But the conger eel was still inside the boat. It was stuck between the seats, with the hook and line in its mouth and it was trying to get loose. It was flapping about wildly all over the place – but my life jacket was right where he was. There was no way I could get it.

Janette

It turned out we were fishing over an old aeroplane wreck from World War II and the water was full of congers. It was dead calm and the water was lovely and meanwhile I went through every stage of emotion from laughing, crying, screaming and praying. I had no idea if Davie would make it to the shore and if someone was going to come and get us or not. It turned out that someone had spotted us from the cliffs with binoculars and had phoned the lifeboat. Lo and behold, we later found out that the lifeboat was delayed getting to us because there was a car parked across their launch and their boat couldn't get out – what idiot parks a car on a lifeboat launch?

When the lifeboat eventually reached us, and they had pulled us out of the water, I was, of course, still topless, and the lifeboat man said to me, 'Well, Wee Jimmy will never be the same to me again.' All the lifeboat guys had been to the show and all the way back they were shouting to me, 'So did you ever find yer mam, Jimmy – or would you rather find your bikini top?' But the crew were great and wrapped me in tinfoil to keep me warm. They hooked the boat up to theirs and towed it, still submerged, back to Peel harbour – with the conger eel still trapped inside the boat.

When we got into port, the lifeboat man asked Ian, 'Do you want this conger?' And Ian was like, 'Nah, it won – let it go.' The lifeboat guy then said, 'You do realise when it gets back to its friends it'll say, 'Honestly, she was this size.'

Ian

So a bloody conger eel sank our beautiful boat. We then discovered that Davie had been dragged off the beach by passers-by after swimming two miles to shore. He was sharing a flat with our drummer and Ron always used to cook Davie's dinner. Ron was always very dry-humoured and when Davie stumbled into the cottage, Ron said, 'Eee, Davie, you're late for your dinner.' And Davie said, 'Ron, you're lucky I'm here at all,' and that was it. He didn't even tell him he'd swum two miles and nearly drowned. He just sat down and had his dinner.

Janette

That night, Davie, who played keyboards, bagpipes and accordion, couldn't stand up straight as he was so stiff from the mammoth swim. But that was the best performance of our lives. We were literally just so happy to be alive.

Ian

Sadly, that wouldn't be our last trouble with boats. In 1984, we had just finished doing a series of summer shows with

Roger De Courcey, The Tiller Girls, Al Dean and Duncan Norvelle when we decided to take my mother on holiday with us on our new boat, *Cape Point*.

One day, Janette, our bass player Harvey Smith and my mother went out on *Cape Point* to Swanage and dropped anchor. It was a glorious afternoon and I went in for a swim, but when I climbed back on board and went down to the front cabin, I noticed that there was something not right – maybe it was the way my shoes floated past me in knee-deep water which alerted my suspicions.

I ran up to the fly deck and told Janette and my mother that we had to head back to land as we'd sprung a 'little leak'. I then called the coastguard on my VHF radio, telling them I was taking on water. The lifeboat operator seemed to recognise my name, as by this time we'd been on the telly for a few years now, and launched boats from Poole, Bournemouth, Swanage, the Isle of Wight – I think they all wanted to see the Krankies drown.

By now, I was feeling deeply embarrassed and decided I would try to save the boat myself, but the water was coming in so fast by this time that all my pumps had packed up as the seawater had wiped out the electrics.

The coastguard crew were now alongside and were telling us to abandon ship. They were concerned that if the boat went down in this particularly deep stretch of water, we would be sucked down with it.

So I passed my mother over to the coastguard first and the lifeboat man then said, 'Bring the child on next.' I was like, 'That's no child – that's my wife!'

I was still determined to save the boat, as it had cost me a bloody fortune, and told them I would try and head for the nearest beach, Studland's Bay, so the coastguard said they would follow us in. I told Harvey to keep his eyes open for any rocks and Janette to keep reading the depth-finder, as I tried to negotiate our way to safety.

But as we approached the beach, I could see my mother staring at the sunbathers. It took me a second to realise that the large crowd that had gathered to watch the rescue operation were all completely nude – we were closing in on a gay nudist beach.

I said to my mother, 'Look at that – a beach full of tools and not a spanner in sight.'

We eventually pumped out the boat, bunged up the hole and were towed back to Poole – and were left with a £7,000 insurance bill. As we had nowhere to stay, we phoned up Roger De Courcey and asked if we could kip with him until our boat was repaired. It wasn't long before he was up to his usual, moaning his face off about anything. I said to him one day, 'Hey, Roger, maybe you should get a boat 'cos we already call you Captain Grumpy.'

7

SUN, SEA ... AND SUCCESS

Ian

In that heatwave summer of 1976 on the Isle of Man, The Grumbleweeds became very good friends of ours. Graeme Grumbleweed is a smashing guy. They did excellent impressions of Tommy Cooper and Elvis and had a mad Scots roadie, Jimmy Gillespie.

Janette

We had an act on our show, this mad Frenchman – an absolute nutter – who did a plate-spinning act with his gorgeous 16-year-old daughter called Chantelle. But this Grumbleweeds' roadie was knocking off Chantelle.

Ian

As I always do with people I'm performing with, I asked this Frenchman if he wanted to come out fishing one day. We were on the boat again when a huge basking shark came past the boat – not uncommon for those waters. In fact, I was used to seeing them all the time as the area is full of them, but this Frenchman suddenly produces a loaded handgun from his jacket and started shooting at the shark. I couldn't believe this nutter was walking around with a real gun. He was seriously off his trolley.

I was so dumbfounded, I was lost for words. All I could muster was, 'There's no need to worry – basking sharks are plankton eaters,' then quickly headed back to port.

Then one day he came up to me and said in his heavy French accent, 'I sinks zat someone is screwing my Chantelle – I sink it is one of the Grumblepersons. I will kill ze Grumblepersons who is screwing my daughter. I shall cut his balls off.'

So I asked The Grumbleweeds, 'Are any of you mucking around with the mad Frenchman's daughter, 'cos he's on to you?' They were all like, 'Nope, not me,' when suddenly the voice of their Scots roadie Jimmy pipes up, 'Well, I've sort of been with her – but she was desperate for it … I couldnae keep her aff me.' I warned Jimmy that the Frenchman had a gun and would shoot him if he caught him.

But that night, Jimmy couldn't help himself and went back to Chantelle's bedroom. Her dad obviously heard them at it and started banging on the door shouting, 'Chantelle, open up – I know you are in there screwing a Grumbleperson.'

Jimmy had obviously paid no attention to my warning and immediately leaped out of the window before the Frenchman burst in. Unfortunately, he fell through a perspex roof outside.

Without a word of a lie, the next day the Frenchman marched into The Lido with his gun out. He started shouting at The Grumbleweeds, 'I know that one of you bastards was screwing my Chantelle last night. Be a man and tell me who did it.' Jimmy was actually standing there with plasters all over his head from falling through the perspex roof outside Chantelle's window, but her dad – being a bit unhinged – hadn't figured this out yet. But as no one owned up, he left again still ranting about killing a 'Grumbleperson'.

It didn't stop there because, the next night, Chantelle's up on stage juggling and she's crap, I mean she's dropping everything – including her knickers as it turned out – all the time.

Our band start putting signs up to the audience behind Chantelle giving odds on when she'd drop the next plate. The audience then started shouting, 'I'll give you £4 at 5-1 …' all of them were having a real laugh, except Chantelle's dad who was still fuming about The Grumblepersons.

I was in the casino on a break having a chat to Maurice Gibb from The Bee Gees – sadly no longer with us after tragically dying on an operating table in January 2003. Maurice was a local boy and a cracking guy to have a beer with and, as we propped up the bar, the next thing we saw was my bass player running past me followed in hot pursuit by the Frenchman who was waving the gun around shouting, 'I'm going to kill you.'

I said to the hotel manager, 'You've got to do something about this Frenchman … he really is going to shoot someone with that gun.'

So the manager did eventually have a word with this loony after he calmed down and convinced him to voluntarily hand in his guns – yes, it turned out he had more than one – to the authorities. He claimed he didn't know he wasn't allowed to walk around with a handgun in this country – although I'm sure *les gendarmes* back home wouldn't allow him to brandish them in the streets threatening to shoot his daughter's lovers either. But the Frenchman and Chantelle went home straight after they were finished, never to have been heard of again.

Janette

We saw everyone on the Isle of Man, from acts like Chuck Berry, Dr Hook, Status Quo and The Bee Gees. They were great performers, every single one of them.

Ian

We did an 18-week season that year, which is a colossal amount of time – now any act would be lucky to get booked for two nights over there – it's sad.

Janette

At that time in our career, we were just having a ball. Every single day was a laugh and we still had no drive to be stars or any of that rubbish. We were earning up to £800 a week in 1976, so why shouldn't we have been enjoying ourselves?

Ian

We also had control of the show and would discover people like Rose Marie, the Irish singer. We only hired Rose because our other singer coming over from Liverpool was caught with dope on the Isle of Man, which was just plain stupid of her as they were still giving the birch for offences like that. So we were stuck for a singer, when I spotted Rose in a bar.

Janette

But we were always up to no good. There was an act over there called The Raffles, who were really prim and proper and quite aloof. So, one night, we replaced their microphones with vibrators.

Ian

That caused a huge barny – they were really upset over that one. They walked on stage and sidled up to the microphone stand not realising that the mics had all been replaced with vibrators – the whole audience were killing themselves laughing.

But we were also on the receiving end of the practical jokers too. Our bass player bought a dead conger eel for the last show and had it pulled on a piece of string across the stage to Janette – it complete freaked her out.

Janette

Last nights were always crazy. Ian used to sing this song, 'Marching Through the Heather', but the bass player gave all the audience bits of heather when they came in and told them to throw it at Ian when he started singing that song – Ian was knee-deep in heather.

After the Isle of Man, we went back to cabaret and that was the first time we did Jollies in Stoke-on-Trent with Ken Dodd.

Ian

Dodd is dead nice man, but his act went on for ever and ever – still does. He just doesn't know when to stop.

I remember one night Ken left a note for us in our dressing

room saying 'Please feel free to help yourself to the drink in my fridge'. We thought that was such a kind gesture and were hoping maybe for a bottle of champagne or such like. But all Ken had left us were two open and half-drunk cans of lager. He's a lovely man but he's always been known for being a bit tight.

Janette

It was a beautiful venue, with fresh fruit and flowers in our dressing room every night and closed-circuit TV so you could see what was happening on stage. It was also a very special venue for Ian and I because that was where we were 'discovered' just two years later.

We still didn't have dancers with us, just a two-piece band, including Davie from the boat incident on the Isle of Man and Ron the drummer.

The following year, in 1977, we were sent to Guernsey for the summer, where we later ended up living for 14 years.

We worked with Brian Paul and Julian Jorge who was a big fat man like an opera singer. There was also a black tap dancer, Joe Chisholm, and four girl dancers. One of those girls married Paul Jones and later went on to star in the big TV hit series *Widows*. Another dancer was Amanda Smith, who was John Smith's daughter – the brewing giant. We didn't know this at the time as she was for ever going shopping to Oxfam during the day and would make a big point of it.

Ian

I remember asking her if she'd ever been to Scotland and Amanda said, 'Oh yes, Daddy has an island in Scotland – he owns Jura.' That was the only time she let on. I asked what her dad thought of her in this business and she said, 'He thinks it's fun and jolly like I do.' So the Smiths were apparently quite happy for their daughter to be working with The Krankies.

Janette

I became good friends with big Julian and one day the two of us went out shopping. We went to cross the road but, because Julian had this huge, fat belly and because I'm so small, when I stepped off the pavement I hadn't seen this car coming. It was honestly eclipsed by the size of Julian's gut. So I was knocked down by a mini. I went right over the bonnet and landed on the road. Luckily, it wasn't going very fast, but I was left in a state of shock.

Strangely, all I could think of doing was getting the dinner in for that night, so after I dusted myself down and told everyone that I was OK, I headed off to the supermarket where I tried to get frozen peas out of the bottom of a big chest freezer – and promptly fell in.

I must have been a bit concussed as the supermarket manager ended up lifting me out of the freezer.

I trudged back home and Ian looked up from his paper and said, 'You've been a while.' I burst into tears and said, 'Oh Ian, first I was knocked down then I was trapped in a freezer.'

He just looked up at me and said, 'You're no safe to go out.'

Janette

By this time, we had a little Sea Nymph, which was 18ft long and had a little cabin so you could get shelter in it. But I never went out that year in Guernsey as I was still too frightened after the Isle of Man incident so Ian used to take out all the men from the other acts for fishing and swimming. He got plenty of use out of it.

It was a wonderful season. The shows didn't finish 'til 1.00am and afterwards we'd go back to someone's house and there'd be singing and dancing all night. It was a fantastic time.

The funny thing is, I always used to read in the tabloids about big showbiz parties with drugs going on, but I can honestly say that no one has ever offered us anything stronger than pot. There was no cocaine snorting or anything like that going on.

Ian

I've discussed this topic with guys like Russ Abbott and he's as baffled as we are about why people take it and even where they're getting it from, because in all our years we've never come across it. I'm sure it must have been more of a London thing.

However, I admit that we were big drinkers. We had rented this gorgeous house, which had peacocks and rabbits in the garden. On the number of occasions I forget to lock the door, we'd come in steaming and the rabbits would be eating the bottom of our bed with a peacock in the corner – I'd be like, 'Is that a peacock in our bedroom – or am I just pished, Janette?'

But apart from those pesky rabbits, I loved the tranquillity of the place and the audiences were superb. The venue would be full of holidaymakers and locals in equal numbers.

Guernsey also had a way of life that was more like the 1950s and we loved every moment of it.

Janette

The booker Brian Paul would hire a ferry three times a season and take the whole show to the Isle of Herm where a buffet and booze was laid on for us. We'd be swimming in this beautiful aquamarine sea. It was idyllic. At the end of that season, we went back to the clubs and, by this time, we were top of the bill in the places we'd started out in, like Talk of the North and Jollies.

It was the manager of Talk of the North, Joe Pullan, who suggested that we enter this competition for the *Club Mirror*, which was a trade paper, where all the club owners put names forward of who they thought was the best club act. Well, he put our name forward and we ended up winning the National Club Act of the Year, Comedy Section.

Princess Margaret was supposed to come to Jollies in Stoke-on-Trent to present the award to us, but she was ill, so Lord Bernard Delfont, the big theatre impresario, came instead, along with the critic Richard Afton from the *Evening Standard*.

When Lord Delfont was shaking our hands and presenting us with the award he said, 'A man called Leslie Dunage from the Isle of Man told me about you two last year. I enjoyed you very much tonight and I hope to see you in London some time soon.'

We honestly didn't think any more about it. But three weeks later, we had to do the show again in Wales for television, which meant Delfont had to come back again to re-enact giving us our award again. That night, we were staying in this country club along with Lord Delfont. We woke up in the morning with a card under our door, which simply read

'Ring Lord D in the morning.'

Ian

He quite matter-of-factly told us we were going to be on *The Royal Variety Show*. But this was February and *The Royal Variety* wasn't until November, so we were sworn to secrecy and weren't to tell anybody at all. That was the most painful ten months of our lives. We were to be Delfont's big surprise and he didn't want anyone knowing. Freddie Starr had been his surprise one year, Rod Hull and Emu had been his big surprise another year – and now that mantle was passed to us.

Janette

We returned to Jersey to work for Jimmy Muir once again – but we simply couldn't tell him that we were doing *The Royal Variety*. It was murder.

Ian

I couldn't even tell my mother because I know she would have told someone in the *Clydebank News* because she was always happy to tell anyone who would listen what her boy was up to next.

At that time, the Channel Islands were attracting the big cabaret acts like The Black Abbots and Jimmy Muir was worried that we wouldn't be able to compete – but we did, and did really well that year.

Janette

We had a very young dancer, Denise Gingell, who was just 16, so we became her guardians as she was just out of school. Denise would actually go on to marry the multi-millionaire record producer and notorious *Pop Idol* judge Pete Waterman. But here she was in our care at that time, which gave us a sense of responsibility. We even became pretty respectable for a while as we'd stopped shagging on the boat and on the golf course.

Ian

This was the year Jimmy put us up in his own apartment, which was gorgeous. But this old Scottish woman who stayed above him phoned up the authorities and said, 'There are gypsies staying in the flat below, they keep coming in at 3.00am.'

We were in this really posh restaurant one Sunday for lunch when Janette spotted this old dear who had complained about us. Well, Janette walked straight over to her table and said, 'Would you like to buy some pegs?'

Then, in September, we were rehearsing at Jimmy Muir's club for the act we were going to put on in the winter, when big Jimmy came screeching up in his Jag and said, 'Wee Janette, wee Janette ... David Jacobs has just been on the radio and has announced you're doing *The Royal Variety*.'

Janette

I was like, 'I know, Jimmy.' He fell silent for a moment then barked, 'Why the hell didn't you bloody tell me? I would have put it on all the bill posters?'

I said, 'That's exactly why we couldn't tell you, Jimmy.'

Ian

It was all over the papers and we did interviews on local TV – it was such a big deal back then. So, after that, Janette went up to this old bitch upstairs and said, 'If we're bloody good enough for the Queen Mother, we're bloody good enough to stay next to you.'

Janette

The last few months of that season we were on a high, drinking champagne and eating oysters every night.

We spared no expense as we wanted to enjoy every second of our big moment. I had a dress made by an Italian dressmaker's on Jersey, and bought a white mink jacket, it was beautiful.

Our main home was still the semi-detached in Coventry, but London agents were now starting to get very interested in us.

Ian

We naïvely thought that they were interested in our career, but they weren't, of course. They just wanted to make money. The only one who was genuinely interested in us was Stan Dallas. We'd met him 15 years before when he was with the Dallas Boys at The Pavilion in Glasgow.

Janette

Stan was phoning us up and saying, 'You have just six minutes in *The Royal Variety* and we need to get new musical arrangements because there's also a 30-piece orchestra. You must time your act to perfection and know exactly what you do.'

He told us to rehearse at any given opportunity, in the house if needs be. I remember one day during rehearsals I was dressed as Wee Jimmy and Ian was in his kilt when there was a knock at the door. It was our insurance man. He must have thought, 'What the hell are these two weirdos into?'

Ian

But disaster struck when I got to the London Palladium. Just when I was about to go out on stage in my kilt for the full dress rehearsal, I was spotted by Andy Stewart, who was a veteran Scottish entertainer, famous for his hit song 'Donald Where's Yer Troosers'. He went to the directors and said, 'I will not have anybody on stage in a kilt before me.'

They came up to me and said, 'You can't wear that outfit.' This was the day before the biggest show of our lives. I was literally in tears. I felt as helpless as a child. I walked out of the theatre in a daze and around the corner into Carnaby Street. I must have been looking so fed up and miserable because, out of the blue, this man said to me, 'What's the matter?' It was like a shoulder to cry on. I told him the whole story – poured my heart out – and he dragged me into his shop.

It turned out he was a tailor and said, 'I will make you an outfit at my expense. It will be an honour to have my clothes on television in front of the Queen Mum.' This tailor made me a beautiful tartan jacket, it was absolutely exquisite. He saved the day for us because there was a gag about tartan in the act that we had so laboriously rehearsed that I would have had to ditch if I wasn't wearing tartan – which would in turn have thrown our timing out.

Andy Stewart had deliberately tried to kibosh me and I never really forgave him for that. I think he was annoyed that we weren't part of the Scottish scene. We hadn't come through the theatres in Scotland like he had and we were Lord Delfont's surprise act – and he didn't like that at all.

Ian

My dad died in 1975 on the operating table having a heart valve replaced. He never got to see us on *The Royal Variety Show*. He always worried about what the hell his son was going to do with his life. So we booked suites at The Savoy for Janette's mum and dad and my mum and brother. But what you have to remember is that Janette's parents were down from a mining village and had never been to London before, never mind The Savoy Hotel.

Janette

I phoned my parents at The Savoy from rehearsals to make sure they were all right and my mum said, 'Aye, everything's fine, Janette … the man's let us into this room – but there's no bed.' I asked if there was another door in the room and she was like, 'Aye, but I didn't want to try it in case it was someone else's room.' I could hear my dad try the other door in the background, then shout, 'Oh, there's a bed in here – and a toilet.'

To be honest, we couldn't really afford to go to such extravagance, but we reckoned it was 'boom or bust'. If it was the best or worst night of our lives, we were still going to celebrate it in some style.

SUN, SEA ... AND SUCCESS

Ian

We spent £2,000 in total, because we also bought two rows at the front of the theatre, which cost £100 a ticket. That was for everyone who'd ever given us work – agents, bookers, the lot, along with family and friends.

Ian

The night itself didn't get off to the best of starts. As I was waiting in the wings, I received my cue to walk on stage just as Danny La Rue was coming off. Danny handed me the microphone and said, 'They're all bastards, darling.' The first thing I saw was the Queen Mother in the royal box, who glanced at me, then checked her programme as if to say, 'Who the hell is this?'

Janette

Then, as I was walking through the audience at the start of the act dressed as Jimmy, I said to this big guy sitting smoking a cigar, 'Excuse me, have you seen me mam?' and he said, 'Oh, for God's sake, speak English.'

Ian

I thought at this point the whole thing was going to go arse up. I quickly composed myself, took a deep breath and announced, 'Sorry, ladies and gentlemen, there seems to be a noise out there in the theatre ...' and they could see me looking at Janette wandering about the aisles. The atmosphere had become almost hostile. Something outrageous had happened. Someone had stopped *The Royal Variety Show* and everyone was craning their necks to look at

95

little Jimmy. I thought, 'If this doesn't work, there's nowhere for me to hide.'

Janette

I was coming through the audience saying, 'Where's me mam? Is this the bingo hall?'

'No, this is the Palladium,' replied Ian.

'That's right – The Palladium Bingo Hall,' I said before adding, 'Are you a group?'

Ian

That was the first big laugh. I knew we had them then. I replied, pointing at Jimmy, 'Has anyone lost … this?'

Janette

We then did a gag that Lord Delfont had told us not to do after seeing us perform it in rehearsals. But I had told him, 'Don't worry … Wee Jimmy will get away with it.'

Ian

The joke went, 'Jimmy, what's five and five?'

Janette

I start using my fingers to count …

Ian

And I say, 'Don't use your fingers.'

Janette

I put my hands in my pockets.

Ian

Again, I say, 'What's five and five?'

Janette

I start rummaging around in my shorts pockets, smile and say, 'Eleven!' The place collapsed in laughter. We had well and truly won them over. We were on a high and also did our ventriloquist act, where I sit on Ian's knee and he throws me about like a dummy.

We then finished with something else we'd also been told never to do, which was not to make any direct reference to the Queen Mother.

Ian

At the end of the act, I said, 'So, have you found your mam?'

Janette

And I looked up at the Royal Box and replied, 'No, but I think I've seen me gran.'

We left the stage with the applause still ringing in our ears, got changed then returned to the wings to watch Gracie Fields, who was the special act that year. As she sang 'Sally', the television cameras caught me with tears running down my cheeks. They were tears of both relief and joy.

Ian

During the royal line-up at the end of the show, The Queen Mother shook my hand and asked where I was from.

'Clydebank, Ma'am,' I replied.

'Oh,' she said, 'I used to go there to launch ships.'

I said something daft like, 'Yes, I used to wave my flag at you.'

She gave me a little smile and moved on to Janette.

Janette

Obviously referring to the ventriloquist act, she said to me, 'You must be made of rubber, my dear – that was wonderful.' All I could do was smile from ear to ear.

Ian

That night, back at The Savoy, we were partying until about 5.00am. We had a great night with everyone. The next day, I'll never forget as the phone started ringing at 8.30am. It was the *Daily Mail* asking me, 'How does it feel to wake up a star?'

Janette

Our heads were thumping, so we didn't exactly feel like stars. Then lots of other calls started coming through – all the papers had wanted us to be outside The Palladium that morning for a photocall. They also wanted to know if it was Gracie Field's voice which had made me start crying during 'Sally' and I was like, 'Nah, it was seeing my dad crying in the fourth row.'

Ian

The morning after, there was a State Visit from the Prime Minister of India so we couldn't even get a taxi to The Palladium and had to get a tube instead. At Oxford Circus, a taxi driver honked his horn at us and said, 'Oi, Jimmy, what's five and five? Bloody brilliant!' before giving us the thumbs-up and driving off. I was baffled. I started thinking, 'How did he know ...?' then I suddenly realised – if a London taxi driver knows who we are, then the papers must be right – we really must have made it.

When we turned the corner, we couldn't believe how many press were waiting for us outside The Palladium. We may have been on a high – but our heads were still banging together.

Ian

The night after *The Royal Variety Show*, we were doing a gig at St Helens Rugby Club and the manager said to us after the gig, 'Right, get your book out so I can get a date for you to come back.'

'Well, you'll have to speak to our manager in London now for all that, ' I said. 'Oh, hit the big time now, have we?' he ranted. 'One bloody appearance on TV and you're too good for us now?'

We had been true to our word and played St Helens right after *The Royal Variety Show*, so he got a full house, but because we didn't know when and if we would be able to come back we were suddenly too big for our boots. There's no pleasing some folk.

Janette

Soon afterwards, we were signed up to do Darlington panto, which was one of the biggest and most prestigious pantos in the country. This was actually our first panto together and we did it with the Scouse comic Stan Boardman who was always going on about 'the Germeens' in his act.

Ian

It was *Cinderella*, put on by a London company called Trends who are a very, very camp company. We were playing The Broker's Men and Stan was Buttons.

Janette

Stan was just full of fun. He was sharing a dressing room with an old actor, Graham Squire, who used to take his boots off between acts but he was so old he couldn't get them back on again. Stan had to help him on with his boots after every single scene. This old actor also used to take up the entire dressing room with all his old make-up tubs leaving Stan about a foot of space to get ready in.

Stan got so fed up that one night he put a sign on the old guy's back, which said, 'Ignore me – I'm nearly dead.' When the old fella walked out on stage everyone fell about laughing.

When he finished his act, old Graham said to us, 'My goodness, I went down a storm tonight – they love me.' So the next scene the old guy had to do, Stan put another sign on him, which said, 'I am now dead', and the place erupted. Stan was always playing tricks.

Ian

Stan was on the TV show *The Comedians* at the time. But he was also famous for being thrown off the Des O'Connor talk show because he told the joke about 'Fokkers to the left of me and Fokkers to the right – and some of those Fokkers were flying Messerschmitts too.' It tragically finished his television career – and to think that nowadays that would be considered tame.

Janette

He kept getting into trouble from the theatre bosses because he was always messing about. One night he collected manure from the ponies in the show and put it in Cinderella's glass slipper. When she put her foot in it all the shit splattered up her leg.

Ian

It was a great season for us because we had become so well known from *The Royal Variety Show*. Even before we opened the panto, they actually extended the run by a further two weeks because of the demand. That's when you know you're on to a winner. We loved it.

Janette

The only thing that was slightly annoying was that the producers were an acting company used to dealing with actors, so they made us do everything to rhythm. If we were walking down a flight of stairs it was 'left, right, left, right ...' and they would berate you in rehearsals for missing a step. They once told me, 'On stage, you would have walked right through a closed door there.' I said, 'Don't worry ... on stage I would have seen the bloody door and opened it as I've never tried to walk through a closed door yet.'

Ian

But it was good fun, even though we were on less money than we were on in Jersey the previous year, when we were earning £1,000 a week. We were top of the bill in that panto and were on £700.

Janette

After we finished the panto in the early part of 1979, we went out to Australia for the first time in the spring. This was because the big, fat opera singer we had worked with in Guernsey was quite big in Australia – well, he was big anywhere as the joke goes – and he'd booked us to work out in Sydney for a month.

Ian

We landed in Sydney where we were invited to do a television programme called *The Mike Walsh Show*. In the four weeks we were there, they ended up getting us on every week. Then his rival Ray Martin, a kind of Aussie Des O'Connor, got us on his lunchtime show. We did six of those and got a great response. *The Royal Variety Show* was also shown the week we arrived, so we became a name Down Under without even really trying.

Janette

The money wasn't great but it was a fantastic experience, relaxing on Bondi beach every day – it was like Jersey with heat.

Ian

After *The Royal Variety Show* was broadcast, they'd be queuing for tickets at three in the afternoon – and we didn't go on until 9.00pm. So what had taken 15 years to build up in Britain happened for us in just one month in Australia. We built up a huge fan base. The only regret was that after that initial first flurry we never returned to Australia until the mid-1980s because we were so busy with *Crackerjack* back home. We left it too late and should have built on that first surge of publicity. We began to make inroads when we returned but if we didn't get on any of the lunchtime TV shows to plug our gigs then no one was really interested.

Janette

We started getting offers in from other clubs, but some of them were pretty rough places, like the Daptoe Dogs race track.

Ian

The compère at Daptoe said to us, 'I will put you on at nine o'clock, then on again at half-ten ... I think.' I was like, 'What do you mean by "I think"?' and he explained that it all depended on how long the dogs would take to run because the compère started the races too. It was literally a case of 'They're off' and then he would run up from the track to introduce us.

This compere told us to do 20 minutes for our first spot. So we did, then he came rushing back from a race and told us to do another 30 minutes, while he went off to start another. He said at no point should we come off stage until he returned as it was our job to keep the crowd entertained. Well, after half an hour there was still no sign of the man. We were thinking, 'Where the hell is he?' as we were running out of material and started doing total rubbish. It turned out there had been a photo finish and he had had to stay behind. It was a shame because we'd had a great night up 'til that point and really won over this new crowd, but as our material dwindled away so did the audience. So a compère-come-race-starter turned out not to be the most ideal arrangement in the world.

But that gig aside, we liked Australia. We only had to adapt our material slightly, changing a few words here and there so they would understand us. We also soon discovered that most venues would not except any swear words whatsoever, especially if there were women in the crowd. Their audiences were very similar to clubs in northern England. They either loved you or hated you, you're either great or crap, there's was no middle ground.

8

WHAT A DOPE!

Janette

We returned from Australia to do the North Pier in Blackpool.
But before that, we did our first cruise-ship performances on
the *Oriana*. We did it for a fortnight, cruising around the
Mediterranean. Tracy Farmer was with us on the cruise. She
had worked as a juvenile dancer with us in Skegness in 1971,
but now she was living in a squat in Stoke Newington in
London. So she left this squat to come on a cruise with us. She
loved living in the lap luxury for a change.

Ian

For our act, I would say, 'Now, where have you been today,
Jimmy?'

Janette

'The Pyramids at Alexandria.'

Ian

'Did you like it? It's one of the seven wonders of the world.'

Janette

'Aye, once you've been you wonder why you bothered.' That got a big laugh because it was so true. We had taken a trip to Alexandria in a horse and cart with this guy who had about three teeth in his head. He was also stinking – the horse smelled better than him. He wanted to take me to see Mohammed's tomb. When we got there, he took me by the hand and tried to take me off to see Mohammed's toilet. I told him, 'There's no way you're dragging Wee Jimmy into any toilet – now bugger off.'

Ian

We had our first and last experience of drugs in Alexandria. The Scots engineer from the ship was telling us they sold good hash there, so I bought £5 worth from a guy in the street who literally had one eye and a big dagger. Before I could negotiate, he'd taken my £5 and thrown the stuff in my hand. I was shitting myself more about taking it back on board, but I had paid a fiver so I didn't want to throw it away. Anyway, I plucked up the courage and sneaked it on board the ship. I asked our musician Davie if he knew how to roll a joint, but all we had was his pipe so we used that. In fact, Davie used to walk around the deck among the passengers smoking this pot – he stank the place out.

The Master-at-Arms even said to me, 'You probably don't know this, but there's someone on board who's been smoking pot – the passengers have said they've smelled it on deck.' I had to prevent myself from bursting out laughing. But I composed myself and said, 'Don't worry, we'll keep our eyes open.' And all the time, it was my fiver's worth of stash.

Janette

I didn't try the pipe as, by this point, someone had found roll-ups. But Dougie, the ship's engineer, tried our stuff and told us we'd bought total garbage, real cheap stuff. He then warned us that the sniffer dogs would be searching the boat at Southampton and the best place to put our stash was in the morgue – as all big cruise liners have a morgue. He said the sniffer dogs won't go near the dead bodies. All the staff hid their stashes there.

Ian

Someone then joked that it'd be some story if we were caught. We were laughing at the headlines

'ROYAL VARIETY SHOW STARS CAUGHT IN DOPE SMUGGLING SCANDAL'. So I thought better of my dope in the morgue and flushed it down the bog instead.

Janette

But a bit of cheap hash, bought from a man with one eye and a dagger, was the strongest it ever got for The Krankies.

Ian

After the cruise, we went to Blackpool and were on the bill with The Black Abbots – Russ Abbott and his group – along with Roy Walker and Les Dennis, who was the opening act. He wasn't very good back then.

Janette

Les was a very light entertainer and did impressions. We got on really well with Russ Abbott though.

Ian

But when we did the handovers, he would claim we'd nicked his jokes. We did the famous 'five plus five' gag and afterwards he'd be like, 'That was mine … I want to use that next time,' for his Boy Scout act.

Janette

We'd say, 'Well, that's your privilege as you're top of the bill, but just remember where you nicked it from because we did it on *The Royal Variety Show* – so people know it's our gag.'

Ian

But Russ went ahead anyway and did our 'five plus five' gag on stage. He only did it the once and realised he'd made a fool of himself as the crowd started murmuring, 'That's The Krankies' gag.'

Janette

To be honest, it was an old gag when we had used it, but it worked brilliantly with Jimmy. Russ was trying to use it in his Boy Scout sketch but, fortunately, he dropped it quickly and we got it back.

Ian

That aside, the show played to 140 consecutive sell-outs. Two shows a night – although that incredible success was in no way reflected in our pay packets. We just thought it was wonderful that Lord Delfont sent us a crate of champagne. That's what you think is great when you're young, of course. Now, I'd be more inclined to say 'Keep your champagne … I'll just have 10 per cent of the box office, then I'll buy my own.'

It would take until 1982 to get a deal like that, which is called 'a tickle' in the trade. Delfont would give us the last two rows of the theatre for ourselves if the venue sold out. So on top of your wages, you got the money from about a hundred seats, which could amount to a fair whack.

But you're naïve at the start and pretty clueless about the people making money from you.

I spent my free time playing golf with Russ and the Black Abbots and Roy Walker who was an excellent player. It was a wonderful time. Blackpool let us join the Royal St Annes for just £70 for the season.

Janette

It was always lovely to go to a town where they really appreciated the acts. We were always going to functions and dinners. We rented a house across from Russ Abbott and, when his wife wasn't there, we used to cook for him. You became very close to the people you were working with because you were with them every day for 23 weeks.

In 1980, we also did the Britannia Pier in Great Yarmouth with Russ. At the end of the season, the local mayor put on a dinner for us all to thank us for being there – but the old codger couldn't remember any of our names. So during his speech he said, 'I'd just like to thank the tremendous acts for coming here this year, including Russ Abbott and his Merry Men … and, of course, The Wankies.'

There were 1,800 people at this function and they were in

hysterics. The mayor's wife was wearing this crimson frock, and her face turned the same colour. We'd been called a few things over the years, but never The Wankies.

Ian

During that time, we did a couple of TV appearances, including Ronnie Corbett's show after he kindly invited us on.

But I soon learned there are 'opportunists' wherever you look in this business. Before we went to Australia, I had put an offer in for an old schoolhouse in Bagington, near Coventry. It was beautiful and we were looking forward to moving in when we returned. But while I was in Australia, I got a phone call to say I'd lost the house – to my lawyer! So, after Blackpool, we didn't have anywhere to stay.

Russ had introduced me to a financial man who sorted us out, thank God, because as an artist it was hard to get a mortgage. One bank manager told me that he didn't feel confident lending me the money because, as he was in amateur dramatics, he knew how unpredictable the business could be. Still, this new adviser got us a mortgage in minutes.

Janette

This guy also told us that we were about to start earning serious money – I don't know how he knew that – but he got us to open a pension fund, which we'd never even thought about. He said it was all going to change when Thatcher came in. And he was right; she changed the entire pension structure when she was elected in 1979. So, in a way, it was Russ Abbott who got us financially sound.

Ian

Janette used to moan at me sometimes, 'Why can we no' buy this and why can we no' buy that – why do we have to stick all this money into a pension fund?' and I said, 'Because, one day we'll no' be famous.'

We always knew that the bubble would burst at some point as it always does. This was even before we had our own television show. I just knew that, one day, we wouldn't be doing this any more. Fortunately, that day hasn't arrived just yet. Don't get me wrong, that philosophy is also what drives so many into this game too. It makes you try harder and to push yourself as far as you can go.

Janette

At the end of 1979, we did the *Babes in the Woods* panto at Bristol's Hippodrome. That was where we met the great Jim Davidson.

Ian

He'd just won *New Faces* and was a total Jack the Lad. In a funny way, he was like a carbon copy of me from ten years before but, whatever it was, we instantly hit it off. I think he always wanted to be Scottish too. His father was a Scot and he loved all things Scottish. He was fascinated about the stories I would tell of growing up in Glasgow. And I loved him because he was so daringly outrageous.

Janette

One night, he came back from London where he'd been filming. All the way back on the train he had been drinking brandy. His opening scene was to enter as Simple Simon on a skateboard. But he was so drunk he couldn't stand, never mind get on the skateboard. That night, we also had this sketch to do with a collapsing bench. Jim had to fall down in front of the school teacher played by Melvin Hayes. Melvin would then shout, 'Get up, Simon,' and Jim would reply, 'No.' Melvin's next line was, 'Why won't you get up, Simon?' And loud as you like, Jim replied, 'Because I'm pissed.' The place erupted in laughter.

Ian

We were playing two robbers every night in front of 2,400 people, on stage with Ben Warris who was one half of a double act who had been bigger than Morecombe and Wise in their heyday. Ben was playing The Sheriff of Nottingham and was a great guy.

But it was Jim who was the real party animal – which suited us fine because back then we liked to party too. We were staying at the Holiday Inn but Jim couldn't stay there as he was banned from all Holiday Inns in Britain after he smashed the front window of one of them. They would let him in for a drink but he wasn't allowed to stay.

Janette

A typical night out with Jim would be to start in The Grapes bar across the road from the theatre and, when that shut, we'd hit the nightclubs. After they shut, we'd then head to our hotel bar until at least 4.00am. We'd be absolutely smashed, but get up the next day for a matinée – it was brilliant.

Ian's brother Alistair came to see us once on his way to

Saudi Arabia on a Monday night and we took him out to a club, not knowing that Monday nights were gay night at this place. There were naked bodies everywhere – beside the bar, jammed in toilet cubicles, absolutely everywhere. Alistair had never seen anything like it and looked worried. Jim said to Alistair, 'Don't worry, mate, just stick with me – you'll be all right.' A couple of minutes later, we looked over at Alistair chatting away to Jim at the bar, unaware that Jim had his trousers and underpants down around his ankles.

Ian

Jim was totally starkers and all the while my brother didn't have a clue – we were pissing ourselves. But that was just Jim. He was a mad bugger. Another night, he said to us, 'Fancy going to Bristol?' It was 2.00am and I was like, 'Who's going to drive us, Jim?' and he said, 'My roadie, Kevin.'

Now Jim had the only roadie in history who didn't have a driver's licence. Jim had already lost his licence through drinking and driving, which also meant he couldn't insure his big Rolls Royce or buy road tax. In fact, his road-tax disc was just a Jethro Tull sticker. So we went through to a nightclub called Chaplains in Torquay, which was a gangsters' haunt. Unknown to me, Jim had been sleeping with the boss's daughter and was a bit apprehensive about going into this place because he had just dumped the girl.

We pulled up outside this place and there was nowhere to park, so Jim just left the Roller in the middle of the street with the hazard lights on and said, 'Let's just go in for one drink and if it's crap we'll go somewhere else.'

I went up to the bar and ordered the drinks and the bar girl

said, 'Don't worry, I'll bring your drinks over to your table.'
She carried the round over to us, then picked up a pint from
her tray and emptied it all over Jim's head – it was the girl
he'd just dumped. Jim was completely soaked through. He
jumped up and shouted a few verbals at her.

Suddenly, these two huge Italian blokes appeared out of
nowhere. The older one said, 'Are you Mr Davidson from the
theatre?'

Despite being soaked, Jim was still full of bravado and said,
'Yeah … what of it?'

The big Italian said, 'You have insulted my daughter and
that means you have insulted me … I'm going to kill you.'

I thought, 'Oh no, here we go.'

Jim needed to say something funny that would maybe
defuse the situation. Instead, he squared up to the big Italian
and said, 'I'm not scared of you.'

The Italian dad just smirked before replying, 'Have you
ever heard of Bristol Mafia? I *am* the Bristol Mafia.'

Most people would have looked to make a quick exit at
this point. But not our Jim, who gives it, 'Yeah … well meet
the Glasgow Mafia,' and he points at me.

I literally looked over my shoulder to see who he was
pointing at before it suddenly dawned he meant me. Well, we
have never run so fast in all our lives. We belted up those
stairs with these two huge Italian men in hot pursuit and
sped away in Jim's roller. Halfway back to the hotel, he
turned to me and said, 'We could have taken them!'

'Jim,' I said, 'I cannae punch my way out of a wet paper
bag.'

'Rubbish, everyone from Glasgow can fight,' he said.

Any night out with Jim was always a fairly unpredictable affair. He was always superb fun – even if he did almost get us murdered by the Bristol Mafia.

Janette

Jim was always one for holding big parties at the theatres, which were always wild affairs. We'd have pyjama parties, ghost parties, where we would tip over stage beds while there was usually a couple having sex in them at the time. All this took place in the theatres and everyone, including all the stagehands, were invited.

Ian

One of the stagehands had got hold of an usherette and had disappeared up to the Royal Box for a quickie. Unbeknown to them, we got the entire cast and crew to sneak up to the circle above them, while Jim and I sneaked into the light box. Just as this stagehand was going full pelt, we turned the spotlight right on them, lighting up his bare white bum going ten to the dozen – the whole place applauded. I don't think that poor wee usherette ever showed her face again in the theatre – if only the audience knew what went on after they left.

Another time, I remember waking up at 3.00am in the bar, suddenly sobering up by this point with Jim in a crumpled heap beside me. He raised his head a little and said, 'Ian, there's nothing to drink, nothing to drink at all.' But I reckoned I could get my arms through a little gap in the shutters of the bar, which I managed to do, and seize a sherry bottle, which Jim and I promptly downed before passing out again. Even today when I see Jim, he still says to me, 'Hey, Mr Krankie, pass me that sherry bottle.'

Janette

We were out drinking and partying nearly every night, something which you can only do when you're young. We were lucky, though, because at the Holiday Inn, where we were staying, there was a pool and a sauna, so you'd force yourself to get up in the morning and sweat out all the alcohol before the matinée in the afternoon.

Ian

That never stopped. We were like that at every panto for the next six years. It was a wild, wild time.

After the Bristol panto finished in early 1980, we went off to America for the first time. We had some money behind us at this point and had always wanted to go to Miami. That was some experience and we stayed in a suite in a top hotel, living like millionaires for a week. But it could be a bit dodgy because that was in the days when the Miami hotels were still all owned by the New York gangsters. I remember asking the receptionist if I could put some money in the hotel safe and the guy said, 'I would hang on to it if I was you.'

'Why?' I asked, because I didn't want to be walking around with all this money.

And he replied matter-of-factly, 'Because the door of our safe was blown off last night.'

Janette

We returned from Miami in March to hit the cabaret circuit

once again. At the time, we were getting pretty big in that scene. In those days, cabaret clubs never had any blue comics or anything like that. In fact, the punters couldn't stand any bad language at all. The blue comics worked more in the Manchester strip clubs. But the cabaret circuit, which we loved, was the type of place you went for a special meal, anniversaries and birthdays, so it was always a great crowd. We had done all those circuits before with Roy Orbinson and Gene Pitney – but now we were actually topping the bill.

Ian

It was incredible to be top of the bill in what we thought were the best clubs in Britain, like Talk of Midlands in Derby, Heart of the Midlands in Nottingham and Night Out, Birmingham. To us, it was a dream come true and it was all thanks to being on *The Royal Variety Show*. Ironically, years later we would lose our top billing because we had gone into children's television.

9

CRACKING TELEVISION

Janette

We were in the middle of an 18-week season doing Great Yarmouth with Russ Abbott in 1980 when we got a call from our manager, Stan Dallas, to say that we had got *Crackerjack*. Our agent Laurie Mansfield had negotiated our contract.

Ian

Everyone in the country knew *Crackerjack*. It had been going so long that even I remembered it as a child. Although, at that point, we didn't realise it was on a slump. It was 23 years old when we took over.

Janette

The strange thing was, we weren't really jumping for joy. I didn't think it would be right for us because Keith Harris had a prime-time show on Saturday night, whereas *Crackerjack* was five-to-five on a Friday night. However, our general apathy disappeared the day we arrived at the BBC studios and realised that they'd spent a lot of money on the show, as it wasn't actually made by children's BBC but by their Light Entertainment department, which had a huge budget. So it was a high-quality programme, with wonderful sets and even its own orchestra.

Ian

I wasn't very happy in our first week, though, as all we were doing was taking over the exact same format from Peter Glaze, Jan Hunt and Bernie Clifton. They were nice enough people but, at the time, Peter was in his 60s and Jan in her 40s – hardly children's presenters. I think the problem with them was that they talked down to the kids and they thought that a custard pie in the face was all they needed to have a laugh.

Janette

Actually, we were in our 30s at the time, which is old in comparison to today's children's presenters, but still a lot younger than our predecessors had been.

Ian

In our second week, I realised something was drastically wrong with the show because the studio audience just wasn't right for us. I asked Robin Nash, who was this ex-RAF commander in charge of BBC Light Entertainment and also had the job of selecting the audience, where he got the kids from and he told me they were all from public schools. So they were all upper-class, plummy kids.

During the second show, Stu Francis, who is originally from

Bolton, asked one of these kids a question during the quiz *Double or Drop*, and the child replied, 'I can't understand a word you are saying ... will you please speak English.'

Stu's face went bright red. I thought he was going to throttle the little brat.

That's when I complained to Robin that the children weren't right for us. They were also still all in their school uniforms and were all a bit cranky themselves as it turned out they had travelled miles in a coach and had not eaten before getting to the studio. So I suggested, 'Why don't you get some working-class kids in from around the corner in Shepherd's Bush?' I got the horrified reply, 'Oh no, we tried that, but they were far too noisy.'

But we put our foot down and the producer agreed and told Robin that it was time to open the door to other children, which was a huge relief. We also realised that we had no black kids or Asian kids, it was all just a bunch of little Timmys and Harriets.

The next week, the entire feel of the show changed. It helped us take *Crackerjack* from 2.5 million viewers to 9.5 million viewers in two years – one of the biggest climbs in television history.

Janette

It was some learning experience. It's not like today where film crews follow they were you around with a camera. Back then there huge big static cameras, and you had to stand in a certain spot and remember which camera you were on. When you were walking across the floor, you had to stop on a certain cross, but you'd be looking for the bloody cross all

the time you were walking. So there were a lot of things we
had to adapt to quickly.

Ian

On top of all that, you had to remember your script, songs
and what to do in the sketches as they didn't have autocue
back then. The BBC was very strict that way. We would get
really mad with them. On a Monday, they would have all
the lighting and sound men come in and they would make
you do the whole show. These dour technicians would never
smile or laugh at anything. All they did was stand there
stony faced, taking notes. They were basically the worst
audience in the world and going through that every week
was very demoralising.

One of the things we used to do in the show was the Good
News and the Bad News. One day in rehearsals, we got so fed
up with these suits just taking notes I said, 'The bad news is
… Jimmy Krankie has no willy,' and Stu Francis said, 'The
good news is … he's got a great big bloody pair of tits.' Again,
we were met with nothing but silence until one of the dour
mob taking notes asked, 'Is that sketch going in?'

Not one of them had a sense of humour. They were a
nightmare. The BBC lot just weren't our type of people at all.
I remember once getting into a lift full of people including
the newsreader Moira Stewart. She was very nice because she
was one of the few who actually said hello to us. When I got
in the lift, I then said something like, 'Going up … ladies'
underwear,' and Moira burst out laughing, but all these BBC
types would be staring at their shoes. I thought to myself, 'To
hell with them,' and I started pointing to one chap in a grey

suit and saying out of the corner of my mouth to Moira, 'That's the head of the BBC comedy unit. Have you met him, Moira? He's a laugh a minute.' Moira was desperately trying not to laugh.

But the television centre at Wood Lane was a miserable place to work. In fact, it was the worst place in the world to try and create comedy.

Ronnie Corbett had told me something that I didn't really believe until I saw it with my own eyes – the writers' and the musicians' rooms at the BBC were in the basement of the building with no windows. The executive suits were on the eighth floor with plush offices and windows with a panoramic view. One of our writers, Russell, was turning into a nervous wreck in that basement. He said, 'They stick me in the corner of a room and tell me to write, but I can't write without a window and staring at four bloody walls.' It was Dickensian.

Ian

Just after we'd started *Crackerjack*, the BBC were always telling us we needed a catchphrase. We actually didn't want a catchphrase as it seemed everyone had one at the time – Little and Large had 'Brill'; Stu Francis had a few, including 'I could jump off a doll's house' and 'I could crush a grape'; even Bruce Forsyth had his 'Give us a twirl' on *The Generation Game*. I was very reluctant because we had always thought 'If you cannae get a laugh – get a catchphrase.' But they were insistent. In fact, every time we went into Television Centre, they would immediately ask if we'd come up with anything yet. It was starting to be a real hassle and a bit of a worry because we'd been racking our brains for weeks, coming up with the truly fantastic yet truly terrible phrases.

One night, we were travelling to a gig at Jollies in Stoke-on-Trent with one of our girl dancers, Karen Long, in the car. We told her our problem and that, despite months and months of trying, we had hopelessly failed to come up with a catchphrase. Karen thought for a second, then simply blurted out 'Fan Dabi Dozi'.

Janette and I both looked at each other in amazement then asked, 'How do you spell that?'

'I don't bleeding know,' Karen replied, 'I've just made it up.'

But we thought we'd give it a try for the first time the following Thursday when we recorded *Crackerjack*. To be honest, we used it in the show and never really thought it had made the slightest bit of impact until about two weeks later when the kid's letters started to arrive saying that 'Wee Jimmy was Fan Dabi Dozi'. We then realised it was getting big when I picked up the *Daily Record* one day and the back page sports headline said something like

SCOTLAND ARE FAN-DABI-DOZI, to go with a match reporting a rare win for our national football team. Even in May 2003, the back pages still used a take on our catchphrase to go with Scotland's defeat to Austria – over 20 years after we first used it.

Janette

Workmen regularly shout 'Fan Dabi Dozi' at me when I'm out in the street. I know some people may have found it really annoying, but I thought it was a great catchphrase. It just sums up 'fantastic' and 'brilliant' in the one word. Karen came up with it over 20 years ago and it still pops up in newspaper headlines or on the radio. So it definitely had staying power and that's the mark of a great catchphrase as far as I'm concerned.

Ian

I would say that the 30-something generation, who grew up with us, actually use it as a general expression. I don't think they're necessarily thinking of us when they use it, but it just became part of their vocabulary. I only wish I'd patented it – but Karen's probably thinking the same.

Janette

Meanwhile, we were still doing the cabaret shows. We'd record *Crackerjack* on a Tuesday, be off Wednesday, back in Thursday, Friday and Monday. We didn't have a flat in London and were still living in Coventry in the Midlands at that time. But we had to do the nightclubs because they'd been booked in advance. So we'd get the 8.00am train on a Monday to London to be in for rehearsals at 10.00am 'til 5.00pm, get the train back to Coventry, have our tea and go out to do late-night cabaret.

We actually needed the cabaret because the wages between us for *Crackerjack* were £500 a week and out of that we had to pay for all our travelling expenses, hotels costs, food, the lot. After that, we were left with nothing. In fact, *Crackerjack* cost us money.

Ian

The one thing the commuting between Coventry, London and Manchester did was stop all the boozing and the parties.

We were too knackered to do anything. We had to be so disciplined and go to bed whenever we could.

Janette

By the end of a 12-week run of TV shows, I would find it hard to concentrate. I honestly thought, 'There's no way I can learn another line.' But somehow we managed.

That season of *Crackerjack* was directed by John Hobbs who had directed *Butterflies* with Wendy Craig and *Some Mothers Do 'Ave 'Em* with Michael Crawford. He was a wonderful director but he looked a bit like a bank manager.

For the next year of *Crackerjack*, they got us a guy called Paul Cianni who directed *Top of the Pops* and *The Kenny Everett Show* and suddenly *Crackerjack* took on an completely different look.

Ian

Paul allowed us much more leeway and would bring out our natural side. It was also Paul's idea that we do the 'Fan Dabi Dozi' record – so it's his fault. As he'd directed *Top of the Pops*, he wanted more music involved in the shows and wanted us to do a pop record too.

At this point, we were getting more and more bands on the show as the viewing figures started to rise, so the record companies would put more and more of their acts forward.

Janette

We recorded the infamous 'Fan Dabi Dozi' at a studio in Haddington, West Lothian, with producer Pete Kerr from Edinburgh and Scots guitarist Duncan Findlay doing the music. But to this day, we have never seen a penny from that record. We did an LP with them too, called *Fan Dabi Dozi*, but shortly after it was released the record company folded – whether we had something to do with that I don't know.

It may be hard to believe, but *Fan Dabi Dozi* was actually our second album as we'd released one independently in 1976 called *Two Sides of the Krankies* – you guessed it, a mickey take of Pink Floyd's *Dark Side of the Moon*.

That first album was made after we'd been approached by the group Lindisfarne's record company. They wanted to venture into comedy and we were to be their first foray. That album was really only sold in the north-east. It didn't do too well, nor did we expect it to, so we bought a load ourselves to sell at our gigs, although we ended up buying more than we could flog.

In 1985, we'd end up doing our third and, thankfully, last album through Polydor. It was another collector's item called *Krankies Go To Hollywood* – ripping off ... well, you know who we were ripping off.

But we never saw money for any of the albums either, or *The Krankies* annuals that the BBC put out every year and which seemed to be extremely popular stocking-fillers. But that's showbusiness. It has a great way of losing money for you everywhere you look. We were always being told, 'Such and such had to be paid and the writer has so much of a cut ...' and on and on.

Janette

At the end of the first year of *Crackerjack*, we were appearing in the *Robin Hood* panto in Nottingham where we couldn't believe the reaction we were getting because of the telly. The kids used to follow us around the streets on our way to rehearsals. They'd be shouting 'Fan Dabi Dozi' at me everywhere I went. It was unbelievable how quickly it had all changed for us. We had a whole new audience right across the entire country.

We'd do two shows a day and three on Saturday because we'd finished *Crackerjack*; we were back having a wild time again. Our home was only 40 minutes away in the car, but we'd usually be having such a great time we'd just stay in Nottingham.

Ian

We had a suite on permanent standby at the Albany Hotel. I'd just phone up and say, 'We'll be staying tonight,' and it was always there for us. We still weren't on a fortune but we did start appreciating the good life. We got a taste for it and wanted more.

Janette

We were working with Roy Hudd during that panto. He was going through a bad patch with his marriage at that time and had met a girl dancer called Debbie during the show.

Ian

When the panto finished, I asked Roy what he was doing next and he sighed and said, 'I'm going on holiday with my wife up to Scotland. We'll have a great time – although you do know I'm a lying bastard.'

Janette

Apparently, before going to Scotland, he was driving through London and his wife asked him to stop so she could pick up a newspaper – Roy saw on the bill poster outside the newsagent's: ROY HUDD'S WIFE SUES FOR DIVORCE.

Ian

He later told us his wife also threw a bucket of water over him at home and said, 'That's what they do to dogs that can't stop mounting.'

Despite his marital problems, he was great fun during panto. He actually used to strip completely naked at the side of the stage every night for costume changes and on the last night an old couple said to me, 'Does Mr Hudd know that everyone sitting in the Royal Box can see him standing naked?' So for 14 weeks, twice a day and three times on a Saturday, everyone in that box had been getting a little sideshow of Roy in the buff!

10

DING DONG

Janette

Showbiz is a notorious graveyard for marriages and people are always curious about how we managed to stick together. Every interviewer on every chat show always tries to ask about our relationship. Jonathan Ross on his BBC TV panel show *It's Only TV But We Like It* in 2002 was typically straightforward when he asked, 'So, Janette, do you dress up as Wee Jimmy for Ian in the bedroom?' I'd heard that one a million times and I just replied, 'Oh no, Jonathan – Ian prefers me to dress as Harry Potter.'

But now in our book we feel it's right to clear up all the myths and rumours. The truth is, we have always been together as a married couple, but that didn't stop us having fun with other people ...

We liked to have fun, especially at these wild parties and we sort of knew what each other was doing and with whom, but we always ended up back in our own hotel suite or in the house together at the end of the night. They were never anything very serious. But it's fair to say that The Krankies were not as pure as the driven snow.

Ian

It was never involved, luvvie-dovey stuff with the others. We never had flings as such. It was just these incredible parties that would get out of hand. Janette might ask someone, 'Where's Ian?' and they would happily tell her I was in the room next door with a dancer with my trousers around my ankles.

Janette

No one took it seriously. It was all just good fun.

Ian

Good, filthy fun. Everyone was up to no good at these parties and we were no different.

Janette

To give you an idea of what we'd get up to, one time we went to this party and Ian put some cottage cheese from the buffet on the end of his willy and sandwiched it with two cream crackers, then proudly announced to everyone 'Look – I'm fucking crackers.'

Ian

After Nottingham, we went out on tour with a show called *The Palm Beach Review* and I remember once running around in the buff wearing nothing but an eggshell on my willy. As I said, I was always stripping off.

Janette

One of the guys in this show was a magician called Eric Zee who looked like Liberace, with a big bouffant hairstyle. He had a real leopard called Scorpio as part of his act. He also had an assistant called Angie and a leopard tamer called Rocky – so Ian had a little 'ding-dong', as we called it, with Angie and I had a little 'ding-dong' with the leopard tamer Rocky.

I used to say to Ian, 'You've been with that Angie again because you have glitter on your balls.'

Ian

And I'd say, 'You smell of cat's piss so I know you've been with Rocky.' But there was never any real jealously between us. If any jealously started to creep in, then it had to stop. We both made sure of that.

I know it may sound strange to people, but showbiz is a very strange way of life. Working in the theatrical world, it wasn't unusual to wake up after a night out with all these people crashed on the floor of our hotel room.

It wasn't just about sex though, that was just something that would happen, it was just about having a laugh with people.

I'll never forget when we got to Glasgow with this show at The Pavilion Theatre and Eric Zee said to me that his leopard needed a run. I asked the theatre manager, Ian Gordon, if it could have a run inside the theatre and I promised him it wouldn't damage any of the seats, as its claws had all been cut and its teeth filed down, so it was fairly safe. Ian reluctantly agreed and told the wee woman who ran his box office – who'd sit there knitting all day in between calls – that she wasn't to allow anyone into the theatre because there was a big cat running around.

This is the God's honest truth – about ten minutes later, a Rentokil man came in to change the mousetraps and said to this wee woman, 'Is it all right if I go in?' and she said, 'Aye, but mind there's a cat running aboot.'

This Rentokil guy walked in, then came running out in a cold sweat shouting, 'CAT! CAT! That's a bloody tiger you've got running about in there.'

This wee woman simply said, 'Aye, I telt ye.'

Janette

The beautiful black singer Patti Boulay was also part of that tour and every place we turned up the newspapers always wanted a picture of Wee Jimmy, Patti and the leopard together. But I used to dread those photocalls as the leopard was always fairly well behaved – until it clapped eyes on Patti; it wanted to rip Patti's head off. So in all those pictures you'd see me and Patti looking very nervous and no wonder.

However, it was at the end of *The Palm Beach Review* that we decided that all the madness and our little 'ding-dongs' with other people were going to have to stop. Because of the position we were now in, there was no way we could get away with it any longer. I mean, workmen were always shouting 'Fan Dabi Dozi' at me from building sites; it wasn't as if I'd be able to keep having 'ding-dongs' with people like leopard tamers quiet for ever.

Ian

It never crossed our mind, at the time, but if the *Sun* or the

News of the World had got hold of that story back then, we would have been finished. We'd have been booted out of television in disgrace.

Janette

I also think there was a little bit of jealously starting to creep in too, and that was no good. We decided to knock it on the head after that tour, after an incident when we returned to our house in Coventry and the back door had jammed, swollen from all the rain. Ian put his elbow through the window pane trying to open the door and cut his arm really badly. We had to rush him to hospital as he'd lost so much blood. On the way there, I remember saying to Ian, 'That's God punishing us for being so naughty.'

Ian

It was just too easy to get carried away with all our 'ding-dongs', which were really just being too self-indulgent. It was living life in excess.

But after cutting my arm, it brought us back down to earth. It took that painful incident to happen in 1981 for us both to get a grip again. We knew we were just getting too carried away and if we weren't careful it was all going to end in a tears. But I swear we have never split up or had a trial separation or any of that nonsense. That has never been an option.

But what we were doing simply had to stop to keep what we have as a couple.

Janette

We were also worried that someone we'd met at these parties

may want to make money out of us, especially when we became a name on TV. We were always expecting some blast from the past to appear in the newspapers saying, 'I bedded Jimmy Krankie.'

There was one stagehand we met years and years later at the Bristol Hippodrome who'd been to all our pyjama parties and The Royal Box incident. We invited him up to the house in Guernsey for dinner and I told him that we'd become a bit paranoid about our past coming back to haunt us.

I'll never forget what this guy said next because it really took me aback. He said, 'Look, Janette, there's no way anyone would have said a thing. We all loved those crazy parties and loved you and Ian. You were great guys and all of us had far too much respect for you.' So I reckon because we always treated people the same, no matter if they were a stagehand or a big star, it probably meant it kept us out of the tabloids even during the height of our years of excess living.

Ian

We would have parties after making our no 'ding-dong' pact together, but we would just be daft. I had stopped taking my clothes off by that point too, and left the stripping to others. A guy called Al Dean joined the show, who was a grade-one nutcase. He'd honestly go up to a woman at a bus stop and say, 'Excuse me, madam, can I see your tits?' The woman would, of course, be outraged and Al would say in his defence, 'I'm not a pervert, I only want to see one of them.' Usually, he was sent packing but he did cost me a tenner when he bet me he'd get a woman to show her tits on Blackpool Pier – lo and behold, he managed it. I don't know what he said to this girl, but she flashed them in broad daylight. I was so surprised because he was the skinniest-looking bugger I've ever seen in my life.

Janette

He was so skinny that during his act he'd put a red balaclava over his head and say to the audience, 'How's this for a match?' He'd then put a black one on and say, 'How's this for a burnt match?'

Ian

I remember a show in Scarborough where we topped the bill. Stu Francis was our support and bottom of the bill was Joe Longthorne. Joe wouldn't really mix with any of us as he's from gypsy stock. He'd pull up outside the theatre and five kids would get of out the boot of his car – no kidding.

Janette

Joe followed me into my dressing room after a show one night and said to me, 'Janette, I really want to give you one.'

I was taking my make-up off and said, 'Oh, do you, Joe? That's nice.'

'Yes,' he said, 'but with you dressed as Jimmy.'

I just called him a silly bugger and told him to clear off. To this day, I don't know if he was being serious or not.

Ian

Joe was a really funny boy on stage, but very quiet and really a bit of a weird guy. And, I assure you, Janette never did take him up on his indecent proposal.

Janette

Also on the bill with us during *The Palm Beach Review* was an act called Nuts 'n' Bolts who were a comedy band with a black singer, but they were all pretty eccentric. They had a thing called a 'bomb tank' – an explosion that would go off in the middle of their act. But once during a matinée in Paignton it never went off.

Ian

It was still smouldering, so they put it out of the window of the theatre and the bloody thing went off. BANG! This is no word of a lie, it was so loud it actually started the yacht race at Brixham. So we unofficially started this prestigious annual event. It was eventually declared a false start, but that didn't stop the bomb squad descending on the theatre. The cops weren't too bloody happy with any of us that day, that's for sure.

For the gigs in Scarborough that year, we had hired a big bungalow where everyone would come to party. One of our dancers, Karen Long – of the 'Fan Dabi Dozi' catchphrase fame – brought her boyfriend over from Ulster one night. He was really into smoking dope. Again, I was a bit paranoid and said to Karen, 'Look, we're now children's TV stars – I simply can't have pot in the house. It would be the end of us.' We also had council officials and theatre managers coming and going to these parties, so she promised that her boyfriend would ditch the dope around us.

One time, I made a huge pot of chilli con carne for 35 people. Stan Boardman turned up with Al Dean and, as usual, within an hour Al had all his clothes off. By this time, everyone ignored him as they were so used to this big bag of bones running around starkers.

But just when you thought Al was calming down, he'd do something so outrageous it would take your breath away. One time, we were all at a function with the Lord Mayor of Yarmouth and Al peed in the mayor's pocket. He had been standing there chatting to the mayor for ages and simply whipped his willy out while they were in deep conversation and peed in his pocket. The mayor never knew. He must have wondered later how on earth he had ended up with a soaking wet jacket.

Back at my party, I was in the kitchen cooking the chilli and everyone else was in the front room watching some sci-fi video. Anyway, I walked in this room to dish out the chilli and the smell of dope would have knocked you out. On top of that, Al was running around in the buff like a madman because he's now high as a kite and he doesn't need any encouragement to go bonkers. Even Karen's old mongrel was lying on its back with its legs lying limp by its side from all the dope. This dog got up to go for a drink and it actually bounced off the walls in the corridor.

Meanwhile, Stan Boardman has taken my chilli and slapped it on Al's arse cheeks, so now he's running around naked with his arse on fire. The stoned dog thinks this is a great laugh and chases after Al, crashing into everything, trying to the lick the chilli off his arse.

I looked at all this mayhem and I just closed the door behind me and went back into the kitchen. I was praying that no one from the council would turn up and, fortunately, they had some emergency meeting that night so we were safe.

But my young brother Colin was there too. He was only 17 at the time and thought it'd be a laugh to take the kitchen sink apart.

Janette

The only problem was, he couldn't put all the plumbing back together again.

Ian

He didn't really care by that point because one of our lovely young dancers took him outside to turn him into a man. We couldn't get that smile off his face for weeks.

When Janette and I got up the next morning, there were bodies lying on every available inch of space. Karen and her boyfriend had slept in the loft on the fibreglass insulation, so they were itching like mad.

But when I left, I got a huge bill from the owners for all the damage we'd caused. The letter also clearly stated that we would never be welcome there again. That was another wake-up call, because I realised that would be a nice little story – KRANKIES WRECK BUNGALOW.

Janette

It was during Scarborough that we really got to know Les Dawson, who was working in Bridlington.

Ian

We'd met him before at the BBC when we were making *Crackerjack*, as he was big pals with Stu Francis. But, in Scarborough, Les offered to have us picked up in his stretch

Mercedes limo and driven to his friend's boat in York. Les was a huge TV star at the time, although, surprisingly, he was by no means the biggest theatre draw. We were packing in the kids and families because we were new and classed as children's entertainers. But Les was playing a smaller theatre in Bridlington, which wasn't the best of venues, and he told us ticket sales weren't brilliant either.

Janette

On this day out, we were with our road manager Eric Getling, Maureen Howden – our head girl dancer – Stu and Les. We got on at York and started the day with smoked trout and champagne. We had to go up all these locks in the canal, where the old women would be waving at Les. He was a gent, although he would always invite the old dears on board, get them pissed as farts on champagne and deposit them slightly worse for wear further up the canal.

Ian

By the time they got off the boat, these old dears would be steaming. Les did it all the time. He was just hysterical. He was always on and would do his whole range of characters all the time. He'd then get bored with that – although we weren't bored at all – and that's when he'd start inviting the pensioners on board. He would be talking to them exactly the way they talked, pretending to adjust his boobs, the whole bit. It's still one of the funniest days of my life.

Janette

I remember he got talking to these two OAPs and asked

them how long they'd been coming to Bridlington and one said, '40 years.' Les was like, '40 years? Why have you been coming to Bridlington for all that time?' And this woman said, 'Because it's flat.' That was gold to Les and he'd use that in his act. He was great at observing people.

We had a fantastic day out with him and, by the end of the afternoon, were pretty pissed ourselves. The only problem was we had a 6.00pm and then a 8.40pm show to do. At about 4.00pm we left York to be driven at breakneck speed in this limo back to the theatre in time.

Ian

We had to drop Les off first and he was so pissed he couldn't find his theatre. Our car had to do a U-turn after Les had got out and he was still walking up and down Bridlington shouting, 'They've moved the bloody theatre.'

Janette

I felt wrecked that night. We hadn't really eaten that much apart from the smoked trout, but we got there just in time. I then phoned Les after our warm-up and asked how he was feeling. He said, 'I think I've been on. But would you bloody believe it, this has been the first night the theatre has been packed and I can't even remember if I did well or not.'

Ian

We vowed we'd never get drunk before a show again. God knows how we got through it. Later, the stage manager said we looked like we were on autopilot and he wasn't far wrong. But it was worth it after spending such a fabulous day with Les. He really was a legend in every sense of the word.

Janette

The Floral Hall, where we were playing in Scarborough, had a very deep pit so the audience couldn't see the orchestra. Maurice Merry – who had worked with Gene Pitney – was the musical director and was great fun. He used to get kind of bored and would do things to try and put us off our stride. One night, he even projected blue movies on to the wall below us, which only the performers could see. He'd put signs up like 'Gobble, gobble, gobble ... does nobody screw any more?', while another time he got this poster of Freddie Starr, cut out his mouth then put his willy through the hole to conduct the band.

Ian

I tell you, some nights you had to be careful not to lose the plot. Imagine what it'd be like walking on to stage and someone is conducting the orchestra with his willy through the mouth of Freddie Starr – showbiz, eh?

Janette

In August, after the summer season, we had to record the new titles for our second series of *Crackerjack* with Chas and Dave who had written the new theme song – 'Get your voices ready, come on hear you shout – it's *Crackerjack*'.

Ian

By this point, the BBC had now gone into a full ethnic drive, so it was compulsory to have ethnic kids in the title sequence, which was a big change from a year ago when our audience was full of white, middle-class brats. However, since we were filming the scenes in Scarborough where we were still working, the BBC told me it was my job to find ethnic kids for the titles. Well, I didn't know any ethnic kids in Scarborough, but they said, '*You* want to film the titles up there – it's *your* job to find some.' Then I remembered, our local doctor was Indian and had a kid. So his boy came along for filming, but because he was the only ethnic face in the crowd we shot the scene ten times and moved him around the pack each time to make it look like we had loads of ethnic kids. No one seemed to notice it was the exact same child.

But when we returned for the second series of *Crackerjack*, a new producer wanted to change everything around. They brought in a lot of fresh blood – two young girl dancers, Lee Miles and Sally Ann Triplet – who were full of enthusiasm and were lots of fun; the kids loved them immediately. They all seemed to work best with Janette, because instead of Wee Jimmy having to work alongside a big glamorous bird, he was now appearing with a couple of bubbly kids – it was perfect for the show. So the sketches suddenly became a lot better and more diverse. We'd do different things like restaurant sketches because, up until then, it had just been things like Robin Hood and all the pantomime stuff, but for telly it should be a lot different.

The result was that the show instantly became funnier. That second series saw ratings soar up to 9.5 million viewers – at five-to-five on a Friday. If a prime-time show gets six million viewers nowadays, it's deemed a huge success.

Janette

I can honestly say, hand on my heart that, although we became so-called 'big names' on TV, it didn't affect as at all. I swear I am the exact same person I've always been since I was a kid in Queenzieburn.

Ian

All that changed was our lifestyle, as we got a flat in London, although that was nothing to do with our pay increase from *Crackerjack*. Despite ratings soaring to nearly ten million, we only got a rise of £100 a week, which meant we were on £300 a week each – pocket change for today's *EastEnders* stars.

However, what it meant to us in real terms was that we were now capable of earning £3,000 a week at the theatre. So the big money was starting to come in from those sources.

Janette

In 1982, we were at the Birmingham Hippodrome with Billy Dante, who was a renowned panto dame. Ian and I were captain and mate doing a slosh scene with Billy, where he had to walk in and shout, 'More paste,' and we'd throw a bucket of paste over his head. Well, one matinée we got the timing wrong and he got the paste full in his face, swallowing half the bucket – suddenly his lunch made a dramatic and unexpected appearance on stage too.

Ian

It came up like a fountain, he was as sick as a dog – but the kids loved it. They thought it was part of the act.

Janette

That summer, Ian said, 'Do you fancy a Roller, Janette?' I didn't because I hate those bloody things. Anyway, he was determined to get one so we went up to this showroom to have a look at a second-hand Rolls Royce. I was trying to put Ian off by saying, 'I'd look stupid in a Roller – I'd need to sit on 20 cushions just to see out the windows.' We then took this horrible, goldie-green coloured Roller for a test drive, to Makro cash and carry, as it happens, so I could pick up some shopping. One of my friends Joan had come with us and she was larking about in the back, waving like the Queen Mother. Joan absolutely loved it. But I was furious. After we'd been to Makro, we went for a Chinese before going on stage that night and I said to Ian, 'I'm not happy with that stupid car – if you buy it, I'm divorcing you.'

That was the one and only time I threatened Ian with divorce. So we never got a Roller and Ian bought a boat instead.

In that summer of 1982, Russ Abbott had left The Black Abbots, so now it was our chance to close the bill. We were on at the North Pier and did two shows a night. The 6.10pm show would come out at 8.20pm, as the 8.40pm audience would start to come in. We used to look out of our dressing-room window at all these people who looked like a colony of ants. It was a beautiful feeling to know they were coming to see us. That was a 1,800-seat venue and we did 120 consecutive sell-outs in one season alone. We did great business there.

Apparently, Paul O'Grady, who plays Lily Savage, did the North Pier years later and he wrote about Blackpool in a newspaper article saying that his favourite memory from the North Pier was the time he met me! I was chuffed to bits when I read that but, to be honest, it was all news to me. He then explained that I was walking up the pier to the show and he got talking to me and, as I was early for the show, apparently we went to a café for a cup of tea. Although I don't remember Paul, I'm honoured he spoke of the incident as I've become a big fan of his over the years as he's an incredible talent.

Paul wasn't the only one to have fond memories of the North Pier though. One year this woman came up to me and said, 'Do you remember me?'

'No,' I replied, because I'm always honest that way and won't try to bluff it. 'From the North Pier from ten years ago.'

I'm racking my brains saying, 'Oh, did you work in the show?'

'No.'

'Did you own a shop on the pier?'

'No.'

She wasn't helping me out at all, so I asked straight out, 'Well, how would I know you then?'

'You walked down the pier with me after a show.'

And that was it. As I said, hundreds of people would speak to us after shows. We'd be signing autograph for 40 minutes after every performance. But if someone like that lady and Paul O'Grady remember talking to us, then I'm just glad we made such a lasting impression on them.

Before our panto season, we went out to northern Germany touring the army bases, performing for the families of the British Forces. We were staying in a lodge near Hanover with two girl dancers including Zoë Nicholas, Bradley Walsh and a contortionist called Fluke. Every base we went to, the Army always cooked a special curry dish for us before the show. After a week, we were sick to death of all these curries so we started stealing Fluke's food because she was a vegan and had everything specially prepared for her – so we all became vegans too.

The mountain lodge where we were staying was lovely. Well, lovely until we burned it down.

One of our dancers was dating our trombone player at the time and one night when they got back for a snuggle in the lounge it was freezing cold so the musician decided to light the fire – unfortunately, the fireplace was just for effect, and had a fake chimney. The smoke filled up the entire lodge, setting off all the alarms; it was so thick you could barely see. Ian and I woke up coughing and the stench was unbelievable.

Ian

The next morning, the German owner arrived and he was furious. It didn't help when Bradley Walsh came down for breakfast singing 'Smoke Gets in Your Eyes'. The German blew up, calling us all hooligans, then he threw us out. In all the confusion, I left behind four suits. So in one part of Germany, The Krankies have been banned.

But we had the last laugh as the owner had set up an honesty box for the booze saying, 'I'll trust you with the bar,' which is the worst thing you can say to a bunch of musicians – it's like a red rag to a bull and they drank him dry.

So we were the perfect house guests, drank all his booze and burned his house down.

Janette

The shows themselves were great to do as all the kids and the families loved to be entertained by acts from home. Then we were always made guests of honour at the regimental dinners afterwards – the Army certainly know how to look after you.

Ian

The troops liked us because we were a family act, but Bradley Walsh was just starting out at the time and didn't quite know what sort of act to do. It was a bit weird as he used to come on with an ironing board and set it up on stage for his act, but not do anything with it. He'd then ask the audience what they wanted to talk about. To be honest, his act didn't work on the army bases. That was the only time we worked with him, so I presume he must have got better.

Janette

We did the panto in 1982 in Oxford with Danny O'Dae, who played the old blind man Eli Duckett in *Last of the Summer Wine*. He must be about 90 now, because he was 70 back then.

I remember every night we used to drag him out. We'd be like, 'Come on, Danny, we're going to the pub then the nightclub,' and he'd say, 'No, I'm going home.' But he would end up coming out with us. It was a really cold winter that year with thick snow and we were staying in the Randolph Hotel and Danny was staying in some B&B up the road.

Ian

We took him to a reggae club one night and he loved it. He was a great character. He told us once about these digs he had in Middlesbrough. The landlady said to him, 'I hear you're playing tonight, Mr O'Dae ... well, I'll know if you're any good in the morning because my next-door neighbour goes to all the shows.'

The next morning, she brought him some tea and toast in bed and said, 'My neighbour said you were very funny last night,' then, without missing a beat, added, 'Do you know, my husband died in that very bed you're sleeping in. He just sat bolt upright, went blue in the face and I knew he'd gone. Anyway, would you like another slice of toast?'

11

THE EGOS HAVE LANDED

Ian

During the 1980s, we would get a lot of guest slots on *Blankety Blank* and *Summer Specials*. In fact, we were on what many people believe was the best ever *Blankety Blank* when the late Kenny Everett bent Terry Wogan's stick microphone in half.

Kenny tended to be so extravagant he took over whenever he was on, and back then we weren't confident enough to butt in, which meant we hardly got to say a word. I would dread when Everett was starring in anything with us as he was so OTT. He got into some bizarre argument with me on screen over a tie. He kind of looked me up and down and said, 'Mmm, a tie – how Sixties.' He really got my back up by saying, 'Are you Scottish? Ah yes, I hear you are still stuck in the Sixties up there.'

Immediately, I knew I didn't like this guy – which Janette could instantly sense. Frankly, I wanted to knock his block off. In fact, during a break in recording, I followed Kenny into the toilet and confronted him. I said, 'I don't like having the piss taken out of me on national TV – you better cool it.'

Kenny immediately melted and said, 'Oh no, darling, I was just having a laugh.' I had worked myself up into a rage at this point and slammed him up against a wall and said, 'Well, I didn't hear anyone laughing.'

He then apologised profusely and we returned to the studio. After that, he was great with us, even gracious – I wonder why? But people like Everett really used to annoy me with their little Scottish jibes. Nothing gets a Scotsman's back up more than someone insulting their country or their accent.

Janette

We never really got to know Terry Wogan though – I don't think many people did, because he never socialised with the guests. He would leave as soon as filming finished. We used to have a lot more fun when Les Dawson took over. He was a great laugh. Ted Rodgers was a lovely man too, whenever we did *3-2-1*. Once, I came on with one of those umbrellas that fitted to your head and a water pump for rain to sing, 'Singing in the Rain'. Unfortunately, Ted got soaked during my little sketch and all the dye in his hair ran down his face.

Ian

But showbiz egos are exceptionally fragile things. I remember once we were performing 'Bigger Isn't Better' from the musical *Barnum* for an ITV *Summer Special* and we really pulled out all the stops for it. We did this circus sketch with stilt walkers, where I was the Ring Master in this beautiful sequinned suit. We also had *It's a Knock Out* wrestlers' costumes that we wore. It looked so good that ITV used us as a promotion clip on the telly. But the Barnum people objected so ITV had to cut it from our act out of the show on the day of transmission.

Janette

It was the first time that I wasn't just doing Jimmy on the telly, and I got to show off my tap-dancing skills and a whole load of other routines; it looked great and we couldn't wait to see the show. But when the *Summer Special* went to air, we could only be seen in the finale dressed as these characters from *Barnum*, so no one got to see us perform. It was so sad watching the TV knowing what had been a great routine had been deliberately cut out. I was very upset.

Ian

Their argument was that it would confuse the public having two Barnums; but how anyone could confuse The Krankies with Michael Crawford is beyond me.

Janette

In 1984, we meet Lena Zavaroni for the first time. She was the Scottish child singer whose young life would come to a tragic end when she wasted away from anorexia. She was managed by a lady called Dorothy Solomon and we did some *Summertime Specials* with Lena. Her manager went everywhere with her because she was so young.

Ian

It turned out Lena knew my brother Alistair because he was

the insurance man from Rothesay on her home island of Bute and had said to her, 'If you ever see Ian and Janette, talk to them,' so she did.

Janette

She was a lovely wee girl. We were playing in Eastbourne with her one night and were going back to London in a car laid on by ITV. I said, 'You can come with us if you want.' And she seemed really excited about that, because we were company for her. But her manager Dorothy said, 'No, Lena, you're coming with me.' I felt sorry for her because she seemed so lonely. Even at that early stage, I think she was showing signs of anorexia as she was getting quite thin.

There was always such a big fuss made over her food. She would never eat in the chuck wagon with the rest of us and she would always go off to eat somewhere else ... that's if she did eat anything at all. She was a deeply unhappy kid, but seemed to light up on the several occasions that we met.

When we did Great Yarmouth in 1983, one day, Ian decided that we should have a beach barbecue at Winston-on-Sea, which is a really quiet spot. Ian prepared all these home-made hamburgers and we arrived around one o'clock with all the dancers and musicians on this lovely summer's day. One of the dancers, Debbie Payne, was seeing the saxophone player, but his long-term girlfriend had just come over from Australia, so Debbie's nose was a bit out of joint. Anyway, at one point she decided she needed a pee and the only place she could go for some privacy was into the rushes. When she came out, she said, 'Something's stung me.' We thought she was just trying to get some attention because she was feeling a bit down at her love rival being at the barbecue too, and anyway Ian had only just started cooking the burgers. About half an hour later, she started going blue in the lips.

Ian

The irony was, her love rival from Australia was a nurse who became very concerned about Debbie – she hadn't a clue Debbie had been off with her boyfriend in her absence. She asked me if there was anything dangerous in this part of the country and I said, 'Naw – you get some adders, but not around here.' By this point, Debbie started to hallucinate, but all the time I was still thinking she was at it.

Janette

But this nurse found two pin-prick bite marks on Debbie's leg and insisted we take her to a hospital.

Ian

I phoned the cops and asked if there were any snakes around there and they told me we shouldn't have even been on the beach at this time of year because it was breeding season for the adders and said, 'Didn't I see the signs?' There were no signs whatsoever.

Janette

We got Debbie into a car and she was sick all the way to the hospital into a Marks & Spencer's bag, but all the sick was leaking through the holes in the bottom. She ended up in hospital for three weeks with anaphylaxis – a severe reaction to the snake venom. The poor girl nearly died. Of course, our musicians were as sensitive as ever and used to throw plastic snakes at her during visiting hours.

Ian

It was in Great Yarmouth that year, we met a guy called Joe Terry who had a company called Magnum Concerts, who promoted people like Paul Young at the time, but wanted to break into comedy. So we went on tour with a singer, four girl dancers, and The Great Soprendo. This guy Joe got us a tour bus and our first job was in Wick on the start of a 48-gig tour. This was no rock 'n' roll tour coach though. It was a right old rickety banger from Oldham with the catchy slogan 'Another One of Alf's' written on the back. But we all travelled in this thing, with an articulated lorry full of lighting and speakers behind us rolling into these wee towns. Joe made a fortune because we were playing wee town halls that he'd rented for two bob and we were on the telly so they were packed out.

One of these gigs was at Greenock Town Hall, which was so dilapidated that the balcony had been condemned. All we were allowed to put up there was one spotlight guy.

Before the show, I nipped out to get some sandwiches and these wee boys were like, 'Hey, mister, where's Jimmy?' They were nice wee scamps and said they couldn't afford a ticket. So I said, 'If you keep quiet, I'll allow the three of you into the balcony to watch the show, but you mustn't say a thing.' When we went on stage, I glanced up and there must have been 150 kids up on the balcony, jumping around. They were swinging on the scaffolding for the lighting rigs and running riot – and all on this balcony, which had been condemned.

The theatre manager wasn't best pleased with me for letting them in.

We also played the Corn Hall in Oban, which only had a cooker and a 13-amp plug – and we were trying to bring in these huge lighting rigs. So this young techie decided to wire up his lights to the power from a street lamp. But when we put all our lights on, it blew out every street light in Oban. This techie crapped himself and ran out into the street to quickly undo his cable before the cops arrived. We ended up doing this show on reduced lights, but it was still too much for the venue's fuse box, which kept tripping. He ended up gaffer-taping the trip switches down, so they couldn't flick off. All the way through our show, we could hear the hum from the electric box grow and grow – I'm surprised he didn't burn the place down.

By this time, I was complaining bitterly to the promoter about the state of the venue in Oban, which didn't even have any seat numbers. But he took me aside and, in a conspiratorial whisper, said, 'It's only cost me £47 to rent the place – and I've taken £4,000 in ticket sales. We don't pay for the electricity either, even though we've used up their year's supply.' So, basically, I kept my mouth shut after that.

Janette and I celebrated our anniversary in Oban and we were deciding on what to do. We were staying in this hotel and I decided – as was my want – to bare my arse in the restaurant. But as I turned round, there was a glass annex full of OAPs staring right at me.

Janette

Even today when we meet dancers who used to work with

us, they still talk about our tours and say they enjoyed some of the best days of their lives on the road with us. They're like our extended family as they all got married, stayed in touch and bring their kids to our shows now, which is lovely.

The musicians and the dancers were like schoolboys and girls, they were always whispering about who they fancied then going off with each other. But some of them met their future husbands and wives on those tours, so no wonder they have fond memories of those times.

Our road manager Eric eventually married our head dancer Maureen. They were probably with us the longest. Eric had been a singer in the panto in Nottingham back in 1980. Prior to that, he was one of George Mitchell's Black and White Minstrels on TV.

He started with us in the summer of 1981, and met Maureen at the Floral Hall in Scarborough that same year. They were with us permanently from that day until the end of 1988, when they quite understandably decided they'd had enough of life on the road and went off to run a little pub in Ludlow together. They remain friends with us to this day and, when we meet up, we still laugh as much as we did when we toured. It was as if it was only yesterday.

Ian

The next year, we repeated that 48-day tour, but this time the promoter – who knew he'd make a load of money out of us – gave us a proper tour bus when we went on the road for the autumn of 1984. In fact, it was Status Quo's tour bus and it was very luxurious with all the mod cons.

It also had loads of bunk beds and, of course, the dancers

and the musicians thought this was heaven – I don't think they were ever out of those beds. They'd joke about how they'd all joined the 3ft-high club.

Janette

Ian and I weren't on the tour bus that year with the 3ft-high club, because Ian became very ill when he suffered a massive haemorrhage one night. That was mainly down to our lifestyle and the fact that Ian has no spleen and we really shouldn't have been hitting the booze so much. We'd also been for a big curry the night before he haemorrhaged. Basically, he had varicose veins in his oesophagus, which he could control through his diet, which we weren't doing. Even an aspirin would make them bleed. That particular night, he'd got up to take paracetamol and had taken aspirin by accident. So that, combined with the boozing and the curry, meant we had to rush into hospital.

We were in the middle of the tour at the time and were due to play Leicester, but had to cancel – something we had never done. That's how serious it was. We only had a couple days off and then, fortunately, he was OK. I suppose he shouldn't have gone back to work so soon but we needed to finish the tour.

After that, he went to see a Harley Street specialist who used laser treatment on the veins. But they bled again in 1990 when we were in Belfast – and again we were in panto and perhaps were overdoing things once more. Ian is a lot more careful these days and he never drinks spirits.

So it was just our luck that we had this incredible tour bus when Ian fell ill – but the rest of them ran riot, drinking and watching blue movies on the video every night.

Ian

It was so frustrating meeting them at the venues and they'd all be coming off the bus giggling and larking around, having a wonderful time, while I felt like death warmed up.

Janette

We had a trombone player, Andy Compton, playing with us in Aylesbury once. They arrived outside the theatre at 6.00am after drinking all through the night. A police horse had just left a huge big pile of shite and Andy jumped out, took his trousers down and squatted above it – everyone took photos.

Ian

It was a blessing that I wasn't on that bus because I think I would have done myself some serious damage. I knew I was drinking too much as, after a gig, we'd hop on the bus and drink through the night until you passed out while travelling to the next gig.

When I went to see the specialist, he had pictures on the wall of himself performing operations on that television show *Your Life in Their Hands*.

He was quite a character, and would look over the top of his little half-moon specs at you. It'd be, 'Ah, Ian Tough from The Krankies, isn't it? Do you fancy a brandy?' Then he went, 'Oh no, sorry, I better not offer you anything like that in your condition.' Like I said, quite a character. Anyway, he sat and listened to me describe my symptoms while taking notes. He then went over my case file and basically said I had varicose veins in my gullet and that I'd have to have them removed.

He then asked me to tell him, in all honesty, what I drink on a week-to-week basis. I actually told the truth, saying, 'Maybe a few beers at night, a bottle of wine with dinner and round off the evening with a few ports.'

'That's not bad for a week,' he said.

'No, no, no …' I said, 'that's not for a week – that's every night.'

He explained that, although I didn't have a drink problem, the problem was my body, and my liver in particular couldn't handle that amount as it was doing the work of two organs with having no spleen.

I asked him if I should quit the drink for good and he said, 'Well, technically, you should quit the drink for good, but you're not going to because you enjoy it. So by all means have a few wines, have a few beers, but what you should never do is binge drink,' which is exactly what I'd been doing. Sometimes I'd go for four days during the week without touching a drop, then the last night of a big show I'd say to everyone, 'Right, let's go and get bevvied.' That's apparently the worst thing anyone can do.

It's a terrible thing that it takes getting ill to give you a fright. I'm just lucky I got the warning and I'd have been an idiot to ignore it, and I didn't drink for a year after that to give myself time to recover. Then I started having a glass of wine or two – good stuff, mind. But the older you get, the less you want to drink anyway. I was also smoking too, but I realised that, with my bronchitis, smoking didn't really suit me, so I quit that too.

Janette

The musicians also keep in touch with us after all these years. They've always told us that they couldn't believe that they had a wilder time being on tour with the bloody Krankies than they ever had being on tour with a rock band.

Ian

They always told us we were madder than these rock stars. They said our parties were better too, because everyone laughed together and no one held court – everyone was treated the same, whereas with these rock guys, they all had massive egos and when they talked you had to listen, which doesn't sound like much fun to me.

12

JOIN THE KLUB

Ian

We were never really aware of how successful *Crackerjack* had become until we were told through the grapevine that Michael Grade – who was head of LWT at the time and now Director General of the BBC – had gone home and said to his children, 'Turn the telly over,' and they said, 'No, we're watching Jimmy Krankie.'

Michael asked, 'Who is Jimmy Krankie?' then sat down and watched the show. Well, the story goes that before the credits started rolling, he had called our agent Laurie Mansfield and said, 'I want the Krankies for LWT – how much do you want?'

Laurie then negotiated £4,000 a week for us instead of the £600 we were getting from the BBC. Apparently, Michael balked at our demands, until he checked our viewing figures and said we'd be perfect for the ITV network on a Saturday night. I tell you, there's nothing quite like being head-hunted to get you a whacking big pay rise.

Janette

ITV put us on at 5.15pm on a Saturday and called it *The Krankies Klub*. David Bell was the producer and he wanted the whole show to be a situation comedy. Russell Lane was our writer, who was also writing *Russ Abbott's Mad House* at the time. But, to be honest, I think working on two big shows was too much for Russell and he was under severe pressure. So we went back to doing more of a variety show with pop groups. We also gave Jimmy Cricket his first regular TV spot.

Ian

We knew Jimmy from years ago, so when the producer asked if we minded Jimmy getting his own slot, we said, 'Not at all.'

Janette

That was during the first year at LWT. For the second year, Bobby Davro got a slot on the show, which proved to be his big break. But that was the last series we did with LWT. I always felt uncomfortable with the producer David Bell who, even though he was Scottish, always had this knack of making me feel very insecure.

Ian

We just knew the show wasn't as good as it had been on the BBC – it certainly wasn't good enough for 5.15pm on a Saturday night.

Janette

The BBC had just spent a fortune buying in *The Dukes of*

Hazard, but *The Krankies Klub* still managed to trounce them in the ratings by 2–1.

Ian

We were still getting between eight and nine million viewers, but that wasn't good enough for ITV who were looking for 18 million viewers. But, regardless, those figures seemed to be good enough for the BBC who thought they'd better rehire us, which was a godsend – although we never told them that.

Janette

The same scenario happened to Morecombe and Wise before us, who had moved to ITV, which proved to be an unsuccessful switch, and then returned to the BBC.

Ian

Funnily enough, at that point Michael Grade moved from LWT to the BBC, too. So after two series and two *Christmas Specials* for LWT, it was back to Wood Lane – and they even gave us more money, with our wages going up to £4,500 a week.

Janette

Although you must remember that that was only for the six weeks of filming – it wasn't £4,500 a week for a year. But it was still a lot better than the £300 each they used to pay us. The BBC did insist, though, that we had a year-long sabbatical from national television when we switched sides again. In the meantime, we did *The Joke Machine*, which was a regional show for Borders TV, so we didn't return to the BBC until 1985.

Ian

The back-up the BBC gave us this time was second to none. They moved us to 5.45pm on a Saturday night, called it *The Krankies Electronik Komik* and shot the whole show on film, which meant it looked quality. They also got us to do location shoots, which meant getting us out and about more. We made mini films for the show like *Mayhem on the Overland Express* – a mickey-take of *Murder on the Orient Express* – and *The Adventures of Jimmy Burgermac*, a send up of John Nettles' hugely popular cop series *Bergerac*.

Janette

It was great working with the producer Paul Cianni again as he made everything fun.

Ian

The main difference I noticed was that LWT was very luvvie, although their hospitality was very good and we always had smashing little parties afterwards in the Green Room. It was a big difference back at the BBC, which was just canteen food, although the quality on screen increased ten-fold. Even our titles on screen were far superior to LWT.

Janette

Our sketches were excellent too, good, cheeky wee plays and I loved doing them. We had two writers, including Morecombe and Wise's scriptwriter Sid Green. The only downside was that all Sid was doing was revamping old *Morecombe and Wise* scripts and giving them to us. He didn't even disguise it very well. He would simply Tippex over the names on the script, but would forget to do even that after the fourth page.

Ian

So you'd be reading 'Ian says
   … Janette says
   … then it'd slip into 'Eric says
   … Ernie says
   … I'd ask, 'Hey, Sid, am I Ernie in this one or Eric?'

Janette

We didn't get on with Sid at all. He really wasn't a very nice person. His material simply didn't suit us and, frankly, we didn't really want Morecombe and Wise's old scripts. It was insulting

Ian

I met a comic, Brian Marshal, in the lifts one day, whom I'd known for years. My mind was preoccupied as I was deeply worried about one of Sid's sketches. I had just been given a bollocking by Sid after I raised my doubts about it and he had told me it was my job to find the laughs and make it funny. He actually reduced Janette to tears that day – as we said, not a very nice man at all.

Anyway, I went off to the pub with Brian to drown my sorrows and, as it turned out, he was doing a bit of writing, so that afternoon he wrote me a sketch called *Toni Macaroni's Café* – that we are still doing to this day.

Janette

Brain had a young family and he knew what tickled his sons, instead of Sid Green who was living in yesteryear. So we told our director, 'We want Brian,' and we got him.

Ian

We had people like Kevin Keegan guest starring and coming into Toni Macaroni's Café to be served by Wee Jimmy. We also had people on like Bananarama, Lisa Stansfield, Shakin' Stevens and Slade, but we'd never really meet the bands as they'd record on a different day, although we did go to the famous Stringfellow's Club with Keegan after filming and he was great fun.

Janette

We also had a great budget of £80,000 a week for *The Electronik Komik* and they made sure they spent every penny. If Ian needed a jumper, the wardrobe people would go to Saville Row to get one.

Ian

They'd spend £300 on a bloody jumper in the 1980s. I didn't even want to wear the stuff, but they had to make sure they used up all the budget or they wouldn't get more next year.

Janette

That's why they took the cast and crew out on location shoots too. One sketch we did was with The Great Soprendo, played by Geoff Durham, who was married to Victoria Wood for years. Victoria came over to Guernsey for a week while we were filming *Burgermac*. The Guernsey Tourist Board took us all out one day as a thank-you for filming on their patch. We had to meet all these pain-in-the-arse councillors at a meal and swap seats after every course so they could get to speak to the whole lot of us.

Ian

One of them said to Victoria – who wasn't really a well-known name at the time – 'My, I bet your husband keeps you amused all the time with his tricks.' Victoria feigned interest and said, 'Oh yes, I'm always laughing,' then this plonker said to her, 'I bet you're the happiest little housewife around.' How to win friends, eh?

Janette

We were that bored with all these stupid councillors that we made our excuses to leave, saying that we had to get up early tomorrow for filming. As soon as we left the restaurant and turned a corner, Ian, Victoria, Geoff and I all started dancing a jig in the car park – only to realise that all these bloody councillors had followed us out and were right behind us.

I worked years later with Victoria when I did an episode of *Dinner Ladies* with Julie Walters, where I played an old Scottish bag woman. It can be strange meeting someone you knew at the start of their career and you always try to see if they've changed. In my opinion, Victoria had changed. She was a very astute business woman and I think she uses that hard business edge to cover up her shyness. She had progressed, but was pretty straight. A nice woman but no edge to her. I don't think she'd have done all those daft things

Ian and I got up to. Geoff always used to have a great laugh with us though.

In 1986, we were doing Sunday in Blackpool and a Tuesday and Wednesday in Great Yarmouth and had our own tour bus to travel between the venues.

Geoff was huge in those days and we'd go buy wine and snacks for the bus trip, but Geoff would buy a whole chicken, saying, 'Just in case we don't get our lunch.' He would eat the chicken by himself, then we'd stop for lunch and he'd eat again.

But one night, Geoff fell asleep on the bus and Ian blacked up his entire face like a Minstrel. Geoff was none the wiser when he went to check in at the hotel reception.

Ian

The receptionist handed over his key in silence, but when he got into the lift he saw the mirror and just burst out laughing. After that, nobody would go to sleep on the bus in case we got them. If you did have 40 winks, you did it with one eye open.

This time around on television we had to make two shows a week and, because of that, we were cramming too much in and I felt the quality suffered a bit.

Janette

I disagree. I thought the quality was fine, but I do agree we were cramming in too much. It was a lot of work, which eventually got to me because I came down with shingles. We had so much to learn for each show that I was obviously under pressure and my body took the brunt of that.

Ian

We had so much to learn that I think we accepted certain sketches we wouldn't have done if we had had more time. We never had the luxury of picking and choosing.

Janette

When that series finished, we went straight back to Guernsey to recover.

Ian

But do you know how they finish with you at the BBC? The only hint you'll get that things are over is when you don't get invited to the BBC Christmas Party. Stanley Baxter insists to this day that he still hasn't officially been told he's finished at the BBC. No one will face you, but you start to notice that certain people begin to avoid you. This happened just after we'd finished the third series and we were looking to see if anyone was going to commission the next one. We needed to know so we could organise our diary for the year – if we're taking a summer season, etc. But the only thing we were told was, 'Go and do your pantomime, come back and we'll have an answer for you.' Of course, as I've said, our invites for the party were obviously lost in the post so we knew something was afoot.

Again, there had been another shift in styles at the BBC. For starters, they were cutting down on the high-budget shows like ours and were also going off using girl dancers and orchestras. Despite all that, they did commission one last series of *The Krankies Electronik Komik* in 1988, before they discovered it was easier and cheaper to make more quiz shows.

Janette

We were probably suffering from a bit of overexposure at that time too. For example, one Saturday night, *The Electronik Komik* was on, then we'd be on *Blankety Blank* and maybe *3-2-1*.

Ian

We thought it was great at the time, not knowing that people would get sick of the sight of us. Also all these other shows insisted Janette appeared as Jimmy, even though our stage act was much more than that. So, basically, Jimmy was everywhere – eventually, even I got sick and tired of switching on the telly only to discover we were on again.

Janette

It wasn't a problem for me, because I've always enjoyed playing Jimmy. I'm not one of these performers who grows to resent the very thing that made them famous. Away from TV, when doing the summer shows, I wasn't just playing Jimmy and would get a shot at something else. I always liked it when, after a show, people would say to me, 'Wow, I didn't know you could play such and such.' While others would come up to me after our live performances and say, 'I liked you best when you played the wee boy.'

But I can completely understand why they only wanted Jimmy on TV because anything else would have confused the children. Many, many children had no idea I was a woman – even though I was credited as Janette Tough at the end.

When I was doing *Crackerjack*, I wasn't allowed to sign autographs dressed as anything but Jimmy, because they wanted to keep the myth going. Once, I did it out of costume and the kids said to me, 'Where's Jimmy?' and I said, 'Well, I'm his sister, I'll sign an autograph for you,' but they didn't like that so I always stuck to being Jimmy after doing *Crackerjack*.

When we returned to the BBC, we decided to buy a place in London, because we were spending £500 a week on hotels.

Ian

We got a flat for £32,000 in Marlybone Road, which was a fortune then, but it was just half a mile from Marble Arch – people would pay £250,000 for that now.

Janette

We told Stu Francis about our wee flat and he said, 'Can I come and stay with you?' We explained it was only a one-bedroom flat but he didn't mind sleeping on our couch. We thought it'd be ideal to rehearse our scripts at night, but we never once bothered our backsides doing any of that as we usually went to the pub. Stu was a great guest though, and would bring us a cuppa every morning in bed, while usually singing along to the radio.

We were still travelling a lot during that time because we were still working the cabaret clubs. One night, we were playing Windsor. Stu would normally come along with us for a drink, but this night he was going to have an early night and asked us politely not to disturb him when we came in. Of course, it was typical of Stu to get bored with the idea of an early night, so he went to the pub as usual and got back to the flat at about 1.00am when he decided he'd give us a surprise. He thought he'd heard us pull up outside, stripped to his underpants, tiptoed out into the street and hid behind a postbox – but the door to the flat slammed shut behind him, leaving him locked outside on a bitterly cold night in the middle of November. Of course, it wasn't us he'd heard at all, so he had to brave the freezing conditions for about 25 minutes until we arrived back.

Ian

He's so cold by this point that he's sobered up and realised that his big surprise wasn't such a good idea after all.

Janette

Another night, we were driving back from Stringfellows in Stu's Mercedes. I was in the front and Ian was in the back with his feet resting between the driver's and passenger's seat. Ian started saying, 'Look at my new Italian shoes, Stu, aren't they class? They cost me a fortune.' Quick as a flash, Stu put down his electric window, grabbed one of Ian's shoes and threw it out on to Marylebone Road.

Ian

It was the wee small hours and there was hardly any traffic around – until just at that precise moment a big articulated lorry turned the corner and ran right over my shoe. Stu was bent over with laughter and I'm in the back wondering, 'What the hell will I do with one shoe?'

Janette

We didn't really go in for the celebrity haunts, except Stringfellow's, where we always went after filming on a

Tuesday. We'd also go to Morton's Wine Bar on a regular basis where we'd meet up with Jim Davidson.

Ian

We got on very well with Peter Stringfellow because we used to work his dad's club in Leeds, so he was always very good to us and insisted on sending a bottle of Dom Perignon over to our table any time we were in.

Janette

We always brought plenty of business with us though, because whoever had been on the show with us, like Bryan Robson or Kevin Keegan, would join us for a drink and Stringy naturally loved having big names like that in his club.

Ian

I remember one night we went to Stringfellow's with Les Dawson, who had just been to visit his wife who was ill in hospital. The place was teeming with press snapping everyone because they had a tip-off that Prince Edward was in there too, which turned out to be a load of nonsense. Les was cuddling the Water Rat's secretary, who was sitting on his lap. It was honestly nothing sleazy or sexual, it was just the way Les always was with people. He'd be doing his act saying, 'Give us a kiss then,' puckering up his lips the way he did on the telly. Anyway, one of the press photographers spotted him and caught him with this young thing on his lap, while Les's wife was in hospital – it would have undoubtedly made the front page.

Les beckoned the snapper over on the pretence he was

going to pose for more shots. Instead, he grabbed the guy's camera from around his neck, opened the back and took out his film and said, 'Next time, bloody ask me first.' The photographer was nearly crying. His big exclusive had just been destroyed in front of him.

Janette

There was this big theatre impresario who lived off Regent's Park. He'd taken a bit of a shine to me and would say, 'I love little women.' His wife had a wee crush on Stu, although it was only flirtation and nothing ever happened about it. This impresario was a heavy smoker, but never flicked his ash, which always spilled down his suit. Every time you saw him, he'd have a trail of ash down the front of his expensive suits.

One night, they invited us all back to his place and he asked Stu to put some music on. His wife then helped Stu pick a record and she started touching his arse. Meanwhile, this impresario got his arm round me and their Chihuahua was shagging Ian's leg – some orgy, eh?

Ian

Although it all came to an abrupt halt when I punted the Chihuahua the full length of the room.

Janette

We quickly left the flat to go back to our place at Marylebone Road, and insisted we would wait outside for a taxi even though it was bloody freezing. It was a beautiful building, which was all floodlit with a fountain in the grounds. Just as the taxi pulled up, Stu pushed Ian into the fountain.

Ian

I was soaked through with freezing water. I shouted at Stu, 'What the hell did you go and do that for?'

'Because you were going to do it to me, ya bastard,' he replied.

And he was right. He must have caught that mischievous look in my eye and hit me with a pre-emptive strike. He was always up to crazy things like that.

Janette

Stu was a keep-fit fanatic and used to go running into work every morning wearing a nylon suit. He thought this meant he could go boozing every night to the wee small hours because he'd be able to sweat it out.

Ian

We played a trick on Stu though, because he was always complaining that he didn't get many fan letters, especially from girls. So I wrote him this letter saying, 'Dear Stu, I have been a fan of yours since I was a little girl. I am now 23 years of age and, if I say so myself, I am quite a pretty girl. I will be in your neck of the woods and wonder if you would consider meeting for a drink and maybe even escort me to my hotel room (I wish! I wish!), yours, etc. etc.'

Stu burst into our dressing room waving my letter around frantically saying, 'Look at this – a bird and she sounds hot.' I'm playing it dead cool saying, 'Are you sure it's for real?' And Stu's like, 'Of course it's for real, just look at the writing and what's she's saying.' So the night he was getting all dressed up to meet her, I thought I'd taken it a bit too far and told him – and he called me all the names under the sun.

Anyway, about a week later, we were coming off the stage at Paignton Festival Theatre at the end of the show, and while we'd been performing Stu had been out for a walk and met a mentally retarded man. This guy had apparently said, 'You're Stu Francis from *Crackerjack*. I've always wanted to meet you.' And Stu said, 'Funnily enough, Ian Krankie has always wanted to meet you – he's heard you've got lots of jokes and he'd like to hear them.'

Stu took this guy to my dressing room, sat him down and left. So when we went into our room after our show, we didn't know what to think of this nice big guy – who, I knew, obviously wasn't the full shilling when he said, 'Stu Francis said you wanted to hear some of my jokes.' I thought, 'The bastard's got me back.' This guy starts telling us all these awful jokes and, of course, we had to listen to them. We couldn't exactly chuck him out. All I could hear from the corridor outside was Stu Francis killing himself laughing. He had well and truly wreaked his revenge.

Janette

Stu was always a brilliant practical joker, but he's also a dear pal. A truly brilliant person.

We were very close to him and his family, and did a lot of summer seasons with him. We watched his kids grow up. His daughter Zoë was just three when we started *Crackerjack* and she used to always quiz me in the canteen about Jimmy, asking if Wee Jimmy was really a mummy – because she knew I was Jimmy and knew I was a woman, she just wasn't too sure how it all worked out.

13

IT'S WIZARD IN OZ

Ian

We returned to Australia for a tour in 1985. That was our first visit to the continent since 1978. But because we'd been away so long, one of the promoters reckoned that no one would remember us so they would need something to draw us in, so he came up with 'The Krankies Knickers 'n' Knockers Show' – complete with topless dancers.

I have no idea how it never made the papers, because in 1985 we were well known as children's entertainers back home and here we were on stage at the South Sydney Junior Leagues Club with boobs flashing everywhere – the dancers', not ours, thankfully.

We later discovered the band The Bachelors were driving past and saw the billboard. One of them joked, 'I can see the headline now – KIDDIES' FAVOURITES CAVORT WITH TOPLESS MODELS.' But we'd signed the contracts to appear, so thought, 'To hell with it.'

The show was exactly as you'd expect in one of these huge Aussie clubs – very raunchy. Wee Jimmy was out on stage working with these big gorgeous topless girls. It was a good excuse for Janette to use all the old lines – 'If you're drowning those puppies, I'll take the one with the pink nose …' and so on. The punters loved it but, then again, they were all pissed and there were birds with their boobs out, so we really couldn't go wrong.

Before the show, we were invited by the committee to join them in a banquet. Now the committees in these rugby league clubs are rather rough-arsed people, as you can imagine.

I got an instant taste of things to come as soon as I walked in the door of this astonishing, grand banqueting room, and they all started shouting, 'Oi, mate, where's the little fart?' referring to Janette. Normally, that's enough to start my fists flying, but there were loads of them and they were all ex-rugby players so I wouldn't have lasted long. Instead, I just groaned to myself, 'This isn't a good sign at all, calling your headlining act "The little fart",' but, as it turned out, it was just a term of endearment and they all instantly took to Janette.

But their bawdy behaviour was in stark contrast to the food – which was literally fit for a king. I had never seen anything like it – silver service, the biggest lobsters ever caught, prawns you wouldn't believe, surrounded by this bunch of barbarians, who were having food fights.

Just when I thought things couldn't get any worse, the chairman jumped up on the table, dropped his pants and put a 20 cent piece between his arse cheeks, hopped the full length of this huge table, and dropped the 20 cents into a pint tumbler. Another committee member then dropped his pants and lit one of his farts with a lighter ... all at a black-tie do, and all in front of the guests and wives.

Janette and I were there with a French girl called Lisa Dore who'd come straight from performing at the Lido in Paris to Australia. She said to us, 'I do not believe zis – zese people are sooo crude.'

I said, 'Shhh – they're paying good money,' but she was right. They were really rough.

The thing is, that's why I like Australia and the Aussies. Here we were, enjoying a meal that could be served at a royal palace, with folk being outrageous and wild – but really enjoying themselves. I think that's why I fit in down there, as I'm a wee bit eccentric like that myself.

Although sometimes that has backfired on me – even in the bawdy land of Australia.

That same year, we'd met up with the singer Tony Christie, who'd had a number of chart hits with slushy love songs in the 1970s like 'I Did What I Did for Maria' and 'Is This the Way to Amarillo?' We went to Manly on a day trip with Tony and we noticed all the workers coming off the boat from Sydney. They looked so miserable trudging off with their briefcases, shirts and ties. So Janette, Tony and I were sitting there having a couple of drinks when I said, 'Look at all these miserable bastards ... come on, let's cheer them up – let's give them a song, guys.'

I decided to do one of Tony's numbers, so got down on one knee in amongst all these office girls and sang, 'Give me your smile and the sunshine in your eyes,' expecting Tony and Janette to join in. I turned round and the two buggers had done a bunk. They were hiding behind a wall, killing themselves laughing. So there I was, in the middle of this pier, serenading these bemused and slightly startled girls.

And it was while we were working in Sydney in 1987 that we came across another well-known Brit. We'd taken some time out one Sunday afternoon to stroll along Watson's Bay. We were just passing the famous fish shop Doyles when someone shouted at the top of his voice, 'Oi, Krankie – I know your brother.'

I'm thinking, 'Who the hell is that?' and turn round to see Billy Connolly on the beach with Pamela Stephenson and their two children.

Janette

I remember the kids were beautiful. Daisy was still in a pram at this point.

Ian

Surprisingly, we'd never met Billy Connolly, and it is true that he really did know my brother Alistair. Billy had met Alistair years and years ago when he went over to Rothesay on the Isle of Bute in Scotland, where Alistair and his wife run the post office. He'd been asked over by Alistair to put on a show to help raise funds to save the local Winter Gardens Theatre, a project with which my brother was hugely involved.

Janette

It was funny that our paths had never crossed until that point, but he was a great laugh and he shouted to his wife, 'Oi, Pamela, c'mere and meet The Krankies,' but I have to say

Pamela wasn't in the least bit interested in the two of us. She sauntered over and meekly said, 'Oh, hello,' and that was it. Billy then asked where we were working and I said, 'At South Sydney Juniors Rugby Club.'

He was dead nice and said, 'I've heard those big clubs are great.'

Then I asked, 'What about you?'

'The Opera House.'

Talk about different leagues.

A few days later, I was having a dress made in Sydney for The Water Rats Ball back in London and the tailor was so proud of his creation he had me parading around this shopping mall in Sydney and, of course, who should be walking along with her babies in the pushchairs but Pamela Stephenson. I'm standing there with this evening frock on with a load of queens surrounding me, making a real spectacle of myself. Pamela was staring at me as if I was some kind of freak show, so I just shrugged my shoulders and I said to Pamela, 'It's just a little number I'm having made for the Water Rats Ball.' She looked at me as if I was mad and snapped, 'For the what?' She didn't even wait for me to explain, she just gave me a little half-smile and moved on. Now everyone in British showbusiness knows the Water Rats Ball. Remember, Pamela may be Australian but she made her name on *Not the Nine O'Clock News* in London, so she would have been well aware of who The Water Rats were. Maybe I'm doing her a disservice and she was just painfully shy, I don't know. I don't know her at all as she only spoke four words to me, despite me trying to be friendly to her. But what I do know was, she simply wasn't interested in even talking to me. I didn't get any nice vibes off her on the two brief occasions we met. I'm just a gab who likes to talk to anyone – and I do mean anyone, no matter their status in life, as that's never interested me. I did get the feeling that she looked down her nose at me.

But she should have known that, at my height, I've been used to that all my life!

That same year we also bumped into Max Bygraves at Sydney Airport. We first met Max at *The Royal Variety Performance* in 1978. He was nice enough but always had a knack of making me feel uncomfortable by patronising me; basically, any time he saw me he'd pat me on the head. We turned up at his home in Bournemouth once in 1986 and he was still patting me on the head. So when I met him in Sydney and he did the same thing again, I just blew my top. I don't know if I was still reeling from the incident with Pamela or that I'd grown much more confident from the first time we'd met, but I snapped back, saying, 'Would you stop patting me on the head every time you meet me – it's very condescending.'

To my surprise, Max apologised profusely, then invited us to his house in Queensland in a place called, wait for it … Nobby's Creek. Only in Australia! It's miles from anywhere and he owns a huge chunk of land – as far as the eye can see.

It's so remote that a cow fell in his swimming pool and drowned once and it took three days for a forklift truck to get there and lift this bloated, stinking beast out of the water.

He's moved from Nobby's Creek and now lives just 500 yards from our apartment in Australia. He's an older man now and we've grown very fond of him. We always invite him for dinner, but as he says, 'I don't do dinner, but I'll come for afternoon tea.' Since then, if he's ever invited out to an opening of a club or casino, he phones us up and we take him there with his wife Blossom – whom I absolutely adore. He's a lovely man too – especially since he stopped patting me on the head.

Ian

Any time he turns up at a casino, he ends up with half the place around him – he was a huge international star after all. But we have a secret signal, which means I have to make excuses like, 'Right, folks, we're up early tomorrow so we have to go,' and Max always mouths the words, 'Thank you,' to me. He's a lovely man and I love spending time with him and hearing stories about how he first started out.

In fact, Max told me a story about when he was young. He used to play gigs in London in the early 1950s with Tommy Cooper. Max used to go on stage first, then they'd walk to the next venue, with Tommy lugging all his props around with him. One night, Max was on stage, waiting for ages for Tommy to turn up, before he finally comes flying through the door. Max was like, 'What the hell happened to you?' Tommy then explained how he was so knackered trying to run from venue to venue he had to have a rest in the street outside a jeweller's shop in Regent's Street. A copper came along and asked what Tommy was doing there. He explained he was a magician, but the copper was having none of it, so he made Tommy open one of his cases to prove it. The bobby still wasn't convinced, so he then made Tommy perform a trick. The thought of big Tommy standing in Regent's Street going, 'Just like that,' cracks me up.

It's so interesting to hear how Max worked his way up from those wee clubs to become a huge star in America. He told us one night how he was at a function once with Jack Benny, Bob Hope and Joan Crawford. Joan got talking to Max, saying, 'Jack tells me you've just played the London Palladium and you're very funny – I must come and see your show.'

'Thanks very much,' Max said, 'and what do you do?'

Well, Joan – one of the biggest movie stars in the world at that time – just looked Max up and down then said, 'Fuck right off,' before turning and leaving.

Jack Benny came over and said, 'Hey, Max – what have you done?'

When Max told him what he'd said, Jack replied, 'I'm not surprised she told you to fuck off – that's Joan Crawford.'

Janette

But every time we meet Max, he's always got another fantastic story to tell us. He told us the Joan Crawford tale the night Ian's brother Alistair and his wife Jean had come over to Australia. They loved having Max for tea and he seemed to have a great night too. In fact, the next day he phoned to say how much he'd enjoyed himself, watching Ian and his brother cook together.

We bought our Australian apartment in 2002. Tweed Heads is a beautiful place right on the border of New South Wales and Queensland beside the Tweed River – nothing like our Tweed river in Scotland as it runs out to wide golden beaches.

We spend around four months a year there, going out

straight after the panto season finishes, so we miss the worst of the British winter and catch the end of the Australian summer. When we're not staying there, we rent it out. After we'd spent our first summer in the new apartment, a lady from Tasmania moved in, who was the perfect tenant as she wanted a long-term let. She was also really cheery and would get up every morning to play golf and wore clothes which were young for her age, so we had no qualms about her moving in. But just before Christmas that year, we had a call from the Australian estate agent saying there had been a small problem with the apartment.

Ian

I'd taken the call and I told the estate agent to cut to the chase. I said, 'What exactly has happened? Has the tenant burned doon the hoose?'

'No,' she said, 'nothing like that, it's just, well, she's died.'

'I'm very sorry to hear that,' I said, surprised, 'she seemed like a such nice woman …'

But the estate agent cut me off, adding, 'Yeah, but that's not all … she died after she hanged herself in your garage.'

Janette

We were left shocked after that call, but Ian broke the tension as usual, when he asked me, 'Do you think she killed herself after finding one of our old videos?'

I was then speaking to John Inman on the phone the next day and he was just as sympathetic saying, 'Ooo, Janette, what happened – didn't she like your curtains? I feel like hanging myself too, every time I see your drapes.'

Ian

Whenever we spent time in Australia, there'd always be a chance of bumping into showbiz pals from back home. We'd met Michael Barrymore on a couple of occasions over the years; the first was around 1986 in Max Bygraves' house in Bournemouth, when Michael was still with his missus Carol. But Michael is not a man you get to know. I reckon if we'd met Michael a hundred times, we wouldn't have got to know him any better. He was a very strange guy and I got the impression that he never truly felt at home with the pros. Maybe it was something to do with the gay secret he was hiding. I don't know what it was, but he was always a very edgy character.

So imagine our surprise when we were on our four-month sabbatical at our holiday home in Australia in 2003 and we saw Barrymore advertised to play our local venue The Twin Towers club.

It's a smashing club and has some great acts on. A few weeks before Barrymore, we'd been to see The New Seekers and Petula Clark who really packed them in and put on fantastic shows. So when Barrymore turned up, we went along more out of curiosity than anything else because I couldn't imagine him packing in the crowds the same way the New Seekers did. Sure enough, when we turned up, Barrymore was playing in front of a half-full auditorium.

As a couple of pros sitting in the audience, it quickly became apparent he hadn't done his homework – a few local gags always go down well, or a few jokes about the area's local neighbours; it's an old trick, but it's something that will instantly endear you to a new audience.

Most of his gags seemed to be about his ex-wife. It was stuff like, 'I was married twice – the first wife died … the second one just won't die.' After that one, a woman in the audience started to cough and he said, 'Don't you croak on me as well,' but by this time the crowd were getting embarrassed.

I just got the impression that Barrymore needed his female dancers and an orchestra for his act, like he had on TV. Instead, it was just him on stage trying to interact with an audience that he didn't know and who didn't know him. He would do that thing he used to do at the start of his TV show, taking the piss out of the crowd. But that fell flat too. Instead, he just rambled around on stage for two hours with no structure to his show whatsoever.

Now Billy Connolly is the master of looking like he has no structure to his shows but, believe me, even a genius like Connolly knows exactly where he's going with his act. He may digress at certain points, but he'll know what he's starting and finishing with. Barrymore was just clueless.

He announced at the start of the show that he had a cold, and he probably did as it was turning into the Australian winter at the time, but that's no excuse. Announcing that at the start of the show is like giving yourself a get-out clause. It's basically saying, 'If I'm crap, then it's not my fault.' But he's supposed to be a professional. Pros work through colds; you have to or you don't get paid. Janette and I have never told an audience if we were feeling under par – they don't want to know or even care. They've paid their money for a night out, they couldn't give a stuff if you're stuffed. Go and feel sorry for yourself after the show, but not in the middle of it.

To be fair, at the end when he came off stage he got a decent round of applause – but the Aussies are always very accommodating like that. It was afterwards in the corridors outside the auditorium that I noticed the difference. It was completely silent. There was no buzz whatsoever, everything just felt flat.

Before the show, we had the stage manager put a note under Barrymore's dressing-room door, saying that we were in the audience, in row such and such. Now any pro in the world – especially ones that you've met before – will invite you in for drinks or a cuppa afterwards. But we heard nothing. He simply didn't want to know, which is unheard of.

Maybe he didn't remember us, maybe he didn't like us, but I suspect maybe he knew he'd been crap and just didn't want to face us – like I said, he was never comfortable in the company of other pros.

A woman from the audience summed up everything when she said to me after the show, 'Isn't it sad to see him like that?' I think that's the worst thing someone could say. If people leaving our shows thought that of us, we'd stop on the spot. But do you know, she was right. It was sad.

I read in the British papers that Barrymore said he was going to immigrate Down Under, probably to New Zealand. Well, I don't know how well he did in New Zealand, but I understand his TV show has been shown there, so he was probably more popular. But if I was him, I'd give Australia a miss.

14

AIR TODAY... GONE TOMORROW

Ian

After we didn't get an invite to the BBC Christmas Party in 1988, I decided to take the bull by the horns and phoned up Harry King at Border TV, whom we'd done *The Joke Machine* with. He was immediately interested, so Janette and I went up there and negotiated the contract ourselves and created *KTV*. This time, we didn't have a studio audience, which meant we could just work to camera and also – as we do in the theatre – we could ad-lib. We filmed it in the borders, up in Dumfries and Galloway, and had a great time as it seemed like the pressure was suddenly off us and we could relax and do what we wanted to. We never heard from the BBC again.

The only positive point we took from our departure was that the BBC didn't replace us with someone else, which meant it wasn't us they didn't want, it was just the end of that style of variety entertainment – for better or for worse. I hope I don't come across as being bitter about the whole situation because I'm honestly not. Everything must change.

Janette

After us, the BBC got rid of Russ Abbott, then Little and Large went, and we were all replaced by game shows. It didn't bother me because I'm such an easy come, easy go type of person – but Russ Abbott and Little and Large were extremely popular shows that the whole family would sit down to watch, so it just seemed daft to get rid of them. They had the ratings that today's Saturday night shows can only dream about.

But that was then and you can't worry about it because television gets rid of everyone in the end.

However, Ian and I had a ball doing *KTV*, which was also networked. It was exactly the sort of telly we had always wanted to do and it was an extremely popular show with huge figures of 5.5 million viewers at quarter past four on a Monday afternoon.

We had great guests too, like Cyril Smith, Bob Holness, Magnus Magnusson and Nick Owen, because whatever shows they were doing we always did a send-up of them.

Ian

The sketch with Nick Owen, who was a racing correspondent, was hysterical. We filmed it at Carlisle races and tried to convince Nick that our pantomime horse would win – Carlisle even held up that day's race meeting so we could film our scenes.

Janette

We did 21 episodes of *KTV* over three years. That was undoubtedly the most fun we'd ever had in television.

Ian

Then the big chop came – political correctness struck and we were out on our ear. They were asking us to explain, 'What is the relationship between this wee boy and the man? And they're a married couple in real life – this isn't right at all.'

Well, I don't believe any of our viewers looked at us in that light at all. We came from a much simpler era. I mean, no one used to bat an eyelid when Morecombe and Wise used to share a bed on screen – now they'd be branded a couple of old queens. Incredible, isn't it? To me, the people who see something sordid in our act are the sordid ones themselves – because they're thinking about it in the first place.

The change happened when Margaret Thatcher put the ITV contracts out to tender and Border lost theirs and were swept up by Granada who, in turn, had to get approval for our series *KTV* from a new children's board. This board consisted of a minister, a psychologist, an ordinary housewife and a TV director, the morality police.

Well, our act obviously went off like a depth-charge in their meetings and that's when we were deemed sleazy or tacky or whatever. We'd gone from having 5.5 million viewers at 4.15pm on Monday to suddenly being out on our arses and all because six anonymous people decided there was something unsavoury about our show.

That's why they've ended up with so many cartoons for children, because, as far as they're concerned, it's safe.

So, in 1991, that was the end of The Krankies as far television was concerned.

Janette

I was sad it all ended, but I get over these things very quickly. And, anyway, we were getting older at that point. You can get away with an awful lot on stage when you start getting on a bit, but the cameras never lie. I would ask the director not to come in too close with the camera because, quite simply, Wee Jimmy was getting a bit wrinkly around the edges.

Ian

We were up against a brick wall with television and there was nowhere left for us to go. It was the same for all the old variety acts. Cannon and Ball couldn't get on television if they murdered someone. Janette and I were in our mid-40s by this point and we had no choice but to turn our back on children's TV and concentrate on the cabaret circuit again.

But even that proved to be tough because we were struggling to get audiences on the cabaret circuit after being children's TV stars. Adults didn't want to turn up to watch a couple of kiddie's telly entertainers.

Janette

It was fine during panto and summer seasons, but you couldn't convince cabaret punters to come and see us. That's really when we became the butt of everyone's joke because the new audiences only saw us as has-been children's entertainers – so from prime-time TV we became the pay-off line for everyone's act.

There's hardly a day goes by when we're not watching the TV and hear our name used. Tony Blackburn even said Rhona Cameron looked like me before he won ITV's *I'm a*

Celebrity, Get Me out of Here in the summer of 2002. But, as I've always said to Ian, these people are doing us a great favour, because at least they are mentioning us. That means our name is still getting bandied around, however derogatorily it's used.

Ian

It's really nice when people come up to us and say, 'Why are you two not still on the telly – there's so much rubbish on.' That happens nearly every day; whether it's just something to get a conversation going, I don't know. But it seems strange that what's on the telly now seems to be the first thing folk want to talk to us about.

Janette

Our agent, Laurie Mansfield, was never concerned when we finished with telly. He always used to say, 'There are people who will come and go, but The Krankies will never be forgotten.'

Ian

I won't pretend that the chop didn't devastate me though. Janette handled it a lot better that I did.

Janette

I've always liked live work better than TV, anyway. So I just said to Ian, 'Oh, forget it, let's go back to what we love best.' So we'd do the summer seasons and panto and would go to Australia for a few months every winter where we've built up a following too.

Janette

It's incredible how things work out, because at the time we were finishing our last *KTV* show for Borders in 1991, my mother took seriously ill and was diagnosed with bowel cancer. We were working at Newcastle in panto with Anita Dobson, so it was quite easy for me to commute up and down to see her.

However, by the time the panto finished my mum was really poorly and Ian and I moved back to Scotland to be with her. We stayed in my parents' old house in Queenzieburn with my dad until my mum passed away with cancer at the age of 76 in the April of 1991. My father by this time was 80 and, because I was an only child, they had no one else to look after them so it was my duty – and my honour – to be there for them both.

The people in Queenzieburn were fantastic and would do anything to help. I remember Ian's Jaguar would be parked outside my parents' house and the kids passing by on their way to school would say, 'Don't touch that motor – it's Jimmy Krankie's.' A wee boy even asked me, 'Jimmy, have ye come home to look after yer mammy?' They were so nice and warm to me when I needed it the most. It felt good to be back home.

Of course, it didn't take long before some journalists started snooping around – well, it was pretty obvious where we were staying with this flash motor sitting outside a wee council house in Queenzieburn. One female reporter rang me at my parents' one day and said to me, 'I understand you've given up work to come home and nurse your mother.'

'That's right,' I said.

She then asked if she could do an interview with me.

'No,' I replied because, for a start, my mother didn't know she had cancer.

I will never forget what this reporter said next. 'Well, when your mother dies, can I come and interview you?'

I burst into a flood of tears and hung up. I have never heard anything so insensitive in all my life. I don't have a big downer on journalists at all, even though many of them have written some pretty nasty things about us in the past. But I wish they would just take a second to stop and think. I wasn't some faceless 'children's TV star'. I was just a daughter who didn't want her mammy to die.

We took the decision not to tell my mum she had cancer under advice from the specialist. He had told us her bowel cancer had spread to her liver but, after an operation to remove some of it and insert a colostomy bag, she would maybe have eight months left to live. I asked after the operation if she would feel OK for a while and the doctor said she would. It was a heart-breaking decision, but I didn't want the time my mum had left to be spent constantly worrying about cancer.

It seemed to work because, after her operation, she really picked up and felt quite well for three months out of the ten she ended up living for. I don't think she would have had that three months' grace if she had been told what was really wrong with her. She would have constantly been worrying about what was to come. Yes, it was a heart-breaking decision, but I think we made the right choice in the end. The thing is, my mum wasn't daft, she knew she was dying, but we never discussed the word cancer with her and I think that's the way she liked it.

My mum was a wonderful patient and, fortunately, was only in hospital for the last five days of her life. My father, Ian and I really helped her get through those months. She was in pain and on morphine, but never complained. Unfortunately, as the morphine doses increased, her personality changed and she started to wander around in a bit of a daze, thinking that no one liked her. But all you could do was take her hand and assure her she was OK. I still miss my mum.

We went back to Guernsey after the funeral and I wanted to take my dad with us, but he wanted to get things tied up with his house. That's probably when those ten hard months really took their toll on me. I had to leave my dad at home by himself for the first time in over 40 years. It broke my heart.

It's horrible how bad things all come along at once – the TV finishing then my mum dying – and it left Ian and I feeling pretty low. My father came to Guernsey and he loved being there and coming out on the boat with us. One day, Ian said, 'How'd you like to sail over to France with us, Bill?' and he was so excited. He was out helping us get through the locks and everything, which worried me sick because I knew he had angina – but he loved it. He used to say to me, 'Janette, sailing is just like posh caravanning.' He was in seventh heaven. We even took him to Spain on holiday where we rented a villa. He'd never really been abroad before and he found it fascinating. He would also join us while we were on tour.

So when we did a summer season at the Gaiety in Ayr, he'd come down to Ayr for three weeks. And when we did Wolverhampton panto at the end of 1991, he came down there for a month too. It gave him a new lease of life.

The Krankies hit Crackerjack!

Top: The late Princess Margaret meets The Krankies and Adam Ant at our first Children's Royal Variety Performance in 1981.

Above: With Jan Michelle and Stu Francis – the 1980 Crackerjack team.

Wee Jimmy gets the measure of Russ Abbott's Cooperman on Blackpool's North Pier.

KTV – TV, Krankies style!

Top: Janette as Miss 'Marbles' for KTV with Peter Goodwright and Willie Ross.

Above: At the races with newsreader Nick Owen and Willie Ross in the last series of KTV.

Opposite: KTV goes to the big top.

Top: In our first panto after our Royal Variety performance 1978–79.

Above: In Pinocchio at the Glasgow Pavilian Theatre with Jimmy Cricket in 1998.

Having fun down under.

Top: Max Bygraves and his wife Blossom have us round for tea at their Australian home.

Above: Ian and Tony Christie in the surf on Bondi Beach.

One of Janette's most recent TV cameos, with Oscar winner Julie Walters, as a bag lady for the 2002 series of Dinner Ladies.

However, after he came to stay with us in Blackpool in 1992 for a month, he went back home in the August and had a stroke. So we'd come up every Sunday to visit him in Stobhill Hospital in Glasgow before driving back down to Blackpool. While in hospital recovering from his stroke, the doctor discovered he also had blood cancer, so we knew he didn't have long to go. When he left hospital, we had him sell his house and come to live with us. Although he was ill, he still came everywhere with us, going to panto in Hull and then, the following year, to Scarborough for the summer season. All our dancers would make a fuss of him as he was such a nice man.

He actually died in Scarborough in 1993 while we worked there. He was so ill by that point, he was always having blood transfusions and would fall over all the time. It was a dreadful shame.

We had three shows a week to put on and rehearse and, during that time, we had to put my dad into a nursing home in Scarborough. It was a beautiful home though, more like a five-star hotel, and my dad loved it. Unfortunately he was so ill, he kept going between the home and hospital before he passed away three weeks later. He was cremated on 28 June 1993, on his 83rd birthday – so he went out on the same day he came in. He would have liked the irony.

This sounds terrible, but my father's death was like a relief in a way – relief for him and relief for me. I'm just glad I got to spend so much time with my parents in the end. I hadn't lived with them since I was 18, and stayed miles away from them. I'd only see them about four times a year, so it was beautiful getting to know them once more.

In truth though, I don't think they would have ever wanted me to have been one of those daughters who stayed at home. I was a little girl from a mining village who ended up living in London and Guernsey and was on the telly and working in the theatre, which I loved. They wanted me to live my own life and I certainly have done that. Had we been contracted to TV at that point, we probably wouldn't have been able to look after him the way we did. So being dropped from the telly had been a blessing.

But I felt really sorry for Ian. I mean, that sort of situation really tests your marriage when you are dragging an ill parent around with you both at work and home, but we got through it and he never once complained.

Ian

We were at a crossroads in our lives anyway, deciding what to do next, so it's funny how it all works out – we ended up with more time on our hands, just when Janette's father needed us the most. Career-wise, though, I was worried, but not too worried because we still had the summer seasons and the panto. I coped by renting an office in St Enoch's Square right in the middle of Glasgow and I used to go there every morning at 10.00am and come back at 4.00pm. I would just spend the day on the phone, calling our bookers, musicians, checking on costumes, the whole bit. That gave me some space and kept me working so we weren't tripping over each other in Janette's parents' house while her mother was ill.

Janette

But since then, we've had no pressure with work whatsoever.

Our years are now divided into four sections

there's the summer section; the panto season; the time of year after Christmas when no one gets any work anyway, so we go off to Australia, do some gigs and play a lot of golf and enjoy the good weather; then we have time at home or doing the cruise ships. It's a very nice lifestyle without having to think, 'Oh God, I wonder if we'll be on telly again,' and 'Oh no, what will we do new this year?' That's all stress. We also work a lot better together because we don't have any stress. If we don't have any work on, then we don't care. We don't have a family to support, it's only us two. No hassle at all – our life is our own.

Ian

There was a really dull spell after that time where we had some pretty shitty jobs and saw a side of the business that we really didn't care for. We were also working our way down the bill, which was hard to take, but you had to accept it. For example, at Blackpool in the summer of 1992, we were the support to Bobby Davro – who, of course, got his break on our TV show. Funny old world, isn't it?

Janette

I didn't care that we were now the support act once again. As I said, it meant the pressure was off and we'd be finished by the first half, then it was off to a restaurant or home. Bobby actually was suffering more than us as he'd just lost his TV variety show too, and was deeply unhappy in his personal life so he wasn't firing on all cylinders. He was going out with Zoë Nicholas for a long time, who was in his show, but he was wanting to finish with her, so his dressing-room door was always shut and he didn't talk to us much.

Ian

That was strange as we'd not only given him his start but had toured with him several times before, but I don't think he was happy with himself at that point in time.

Janette

Since then, he's been great with us again – he was obviously just going through a bad time.

Ian

However, we had a superb season as The Grand in Blackpool is a fantastic venue and we really packed it in. All we did was 17 minutes in the show then we would play a round of golf or relax at our rented cottage, which was on the grounds of this big estate owned by Jimmy Porter and Len Rawcliffe who owned lots of B&Bs in the area. They'd done an incredible job of doing this place up so we had the run of 12 acres where you could see deer and even llamas wandering free.

Janette

There was a big swimming pool, which we used all the time. It was very tranquil, very relaxing and just perfect – and we got to enjoy all that for working just 17 minutes a day.

The manager of The Grand Theatre, Paul Isles, was then hired to run the new Festival Theatre in Edinburgh and he said to us on the last night that when he opened in Edinburgh he wanted to stage the biggest variety show seen in Scotland in years – and he wanted us to close the bill.

He really did seem to be taken with us. Unfortunately for him, the chattering classes in Edinburgh didn't like his idea of bringing The Krankies to town and they slaughtered him in the press. Even the local councillor, Nolan, went ballistic about it. He went on TV and said, 'The Krankies were only fit for backstreet concerts in Craigmiller,' which was a bit harsh on the people of Craigmiller.

Ian

We were flooded with calls from all the papers like *The Scotsman* and STV wanting our comments, which we gladly gave.

Janette

Nolan came out with some classic quotes though. He said that the Festival Theatre shouldn't be opened with a variety show, it should be The Three Tenors – well, you would need more than three tenners to see Domingo and his mates compared to the £12 we were charging.

Ian

When we finished the show, I apologised to the audience that the Three Tenors couldn't make it tonight, because they were playing Craigmiller's Miner's Welfare Club – the place erupted in hysterics.

Janette

The next morning, we were driving back to Guernsey and there was a phone-in on some radio show and Councillor Nolan was in the studio, and we were also taking part on our mobile phone. Nolan said to us, 'I never watched you last night, but I heard had it not been for me you wouldn't have had any material for your act.' I just said, 'I know, Councillor Nolan, it amazes us just how we've managed to survive in this business for so long without you.'

15

LOOK WHO'S STALKING

Janette

In 1990, we were at The Theatre Royal in Newcastle where we topped the bill in *Aladdin* with Anita Dobson and Bernard Bresslaw from the *Carry On* films.

One night, I came out of the stage door with Anita to find what we thought was a child waiting on her own for an autograph. I spoke to her and realised it was a small woman in her 20s.

She seemed infatuated with us and asked where Ian had gone. No surprise to know he'd nipped off to the pub across the road with Bernard and our director Russell Lane. She told me she didn't have anywhere to stay and started shaking and crying and working herself up into a pretty distressed state. It turned out that, just before I'd met her, she had asked the stage doorman where we lived but he wouldn't tell her and that's when she began to get upset.

So I took her to the police station and, by this time, I'd

sussed that this girl was not quite right and seemed to have the mind of a kid and not someone her age. The police contacted her parents in Derby and they came up and collected her the next day.

We thought no more of this until she turned up the next year at the panto in Wolverhampton. She would wait outside the stage door almost every night, so I got hold of her mother's phone number and told her where her daughter was. Her mum was very apologetic and I'd phone them every time their daughter turned up outside the stage door. They would always come to get her and take her back home, but a few nights later she'd always be back waiting for Ian and me.

Her behaviour was starting to get more and more disturbing. One time, she was found walking along the motorway by the police and when she talked to me she seemed very interested in how I, being small like herself, had managed to marry Ian. Then she wanted to know why I was on stage and, more to the point, why she wasn't.

She then appeared again at Blackpool that summer, staying outside the stage door for two solid weeks, standing outside every night asking if she could come into our dressing room. I would tell her, 'No,' and that she should really be back at home with her mother, because she'd be worried sick. That's when she started getting rather nasty and began writing me very disturbing letters saying she was in love with Ian and was going to kill me.

Ian

These letters had gone beyond a joke. Janette had been nothing but kind to this girl, but now she was deeply distressing Janette. I phoned the girl's parents again who then told us they feared this would happen as their daughter had had a fixation on us since she was very young. They were at their wits' end themselves and had obviously been through the wringer with their daughter, but they promised they would collect her and take her to a doctor.

But it still didn't stop there and, for our next shows at The New Theatre in Hull, she turned up again. I had anticipated it this time and warned the theatre staff that this girl may turn up and ask for our personal details as she was harassing Janette. I showed the letters she had been writing to Janette to the theatre's management and told them to look out for her.

Sure enough, she turned up once again, saying to the theatre staff that she had nowhere to stay, but Janette would look after her. This time, the theatre phoned her mother and the police.

But, somehow, this girl had got into the auditorium after our matinée performance and threatened to jump off the circle if she wasn't allowed to marry me. The police talked her down and the theatre manager phoned her mum and dad to come and collect her, but as the manager was putting her into their car, she jumped out just as they were driving off. The police later caught her and told the parents that she would be certified if they didn't seek urgent medical help for their daughter themselves.

Again, we thought we'd heard the last of it but, oh no, this girl was persistent. The following summer in Scarborough, she turned up once more, but with a change of tactic, saying she had come to apologise, as she had been in a hospital to have treatment to get over her infatuation with Janette and me. But no sooner had she apologised, she started to tell Janette that she should let me marry her. I thought, 'Well, that was a waste of a year's worth of therapy.'

Janette had come to the end of her tether. This campaign had gone on for over two years now. I wouldn't say we lived in fear, but every time you came out of a show you were expecting this girl to be there – and she usually was. With someone that unstable you just never know what they are going to do. She had already threatened to kill Janette so she'd obviously dreamed of doing something nasty to her.

On this occasion, Janette just snapped and told the girl to get lost. She then marched back inside the theatre and called the police, told them the story and this time they arrived with a doctor who certified the girl on the spot. It's sad that it had to end like that, but she left us with little choice. Someone like that begins to cast a shadow over your life and, if you're not careful, they can end up taking over.

The last thing we ever heard from her was a letter she sent to us, saying that she'd never bother us again, as she'd once talked to Ken Dodd in Blackpool and was going to follow him from now on instead. We thought, 'Good luck, Ken.'

Janette

But you can imagine our hearts were in our mouths when we read in May 2003 how Ken Dodd and his girlfriend had been subjected to years of threatening behaviour from one of Ken's obsessed fans. The court case had said that this girl thought Ken's girlfriend was standing in the way of a relationship with him – it had all the hallmarks of my stalker. Incredibly, it turned out to be a different girl. So, who knows,

Ken may have ended up with our stalker and this other one. Poor guy. But I dread to think what would have happened if it had carried on because, obviously, in Ken's case, things can get extremely out of hand, and what starts as something slightly annoying can escalate into something that takes over your life.

One way of avoiding the hassle of stage-door stalkers is to run away to sea, which is what we did in May of 1994. We were working in Perth, Western Australia, when we were approached by Cunard asking if we'd take a stint on the *QEII*, travelling from Southampton to the Mediterranean. We'd hadn't worked on any ships since the *Oriana* years before and, being the prestigious *QEII*, we naturally jumped at the chance.

We were queuing up to get on board with the rest of passengers and behind us were two old ladies from Edinburgh. One of them said out loud, 'What are you two doing on here?'

I was going to ignore them, as I could tell from her tone of voice she wasn't even trying to be polite, but instead I turned round, smiled and said, 'We're the cabaret for this cruise.'

Well, she looked as if I'd just shat in her handbag. Both their jaws dropped to the floor and they shouted in unison, '*You're* the cabaret – on the *QEII*?'

'Why?' I said, 'who were you expecting – Shirley bleeding Bassey?'

With that they marched off, shaking their heads and muttering to each other, probably along the lines of the standards on the *QEII* have really dropped since the last time they were on board.

Ian

The thing is, we always talk to anybody, but we'd scared off these two old snobs just by our presence. The next day, I got chatting to the first engineer who, it turned out, had been at school with me in Clydebank. He then told us that the night before, these two old dears had been sitting at the Captain's table and when he asked them if they had been enjoying the cruise. They replied, 'Oh, it's marvellous, this is our fifth trip – but we were rather shocked to see that you had Glasgow comedians on board. I mean, what's the *QEII* come to using Glasgow comedians?'

The captain then asked, 'Well, have you been to see them?' and their reply summed it up when one of them said, 'Oh no, we're not ones for laughing.'

But it's nice to see that the old Glasgow–Edinburgh rivalry is still going strong.

Janette

Jack Tinker, who'd been the *Daily Mail*'s showbiz critic for years, was on board for this trip, along with the comic Jim Bowen, and we all instantly hit it off. Jim told us some great stories, including one about two Scots contestants he once had on his TV show *Bullseye*. These two guys had won everything on the show, from the boat to the caravan, and had gone on a bender to celebrate. Eventually, they passed out drunk in the hotel where *Bullseye* had put them up. But one of them had got up for a shit during the night and hadn't quite made it to the toilet and had crapped in a corner of the hotel bedroom instead. This contestant decided to try and get rid of the mess and seemed to remember seeing a Hoover down the corridor. So he nipped down, got the

Hoover and ran it over his pile of crap. Unfortunately, it wasn't actually a Hoover – it was a floor polisher and it sent the shit spraying over every wall in the room.

Ian

Jim was a great laugh and every night we'd sit in the bar swapping stories.

Janette

However, just a few days into the trip, we were hit with this awful storm. It was getting pretty violent around midnight as we were all sitting in the bar together. Then I noticed a really old woman with a Zimmer frame trying to make her way along to her cabin. It ended up I got lumbered with her as all the staff are quite fly and when they see an old doddery person, they're experts at making themselves scarce. It took me ages to take her along to her cabin. It was getting really rough at this point and, as we made our painfully slow way through a dining room, all the crockery was smashing on the ground. The woman kept saying, 'I'm going to be sick,' but I managed to coax her along and eventually got her to her room.

By the time I came back, it seemed like I'd been away for hours, and I told Jim and Ian how I'd had to put this woman to bed, taken off her knickers and everything – they were killing themselves.

The next morning, when we saw Jim at breakfast, he said, 'Janette, I spoke to that old woman you helped last night and she was so grateful for what you did – but she's just wondering what happened to her jewellery.'

Ian

The only drawback about this trip was that there were 70 amateur magicians on board having a convention – it was like being in the company of Paul Daniels, only 70 times worse. It was terrible. You couldn't walk anywhere without one of them trying to show you card tricks or pull flowers from your ears. They were starting to really annoy us but, unlike Paul Daniels, there were so many of them I couldn't go around punching all their lights out.

Janette

This magician came up to me at the bar one night when I was in the middle of a conversation with Jack and demanded, 'Pick a card.' I was like, 'I'm actually talking to someone,' but he was most insistent and said, 'Pick a card … it won't take long.' So I did that and he then said, 'Now sit on it.' So I did that too, to keep him happy and he then said, 'If I told you that you were sitting on the ace of spades, what would you say?' I replied, 'I'd say you know more than my gynaecologist.' He didn't like that reply so he skulked away, before returning about 15 minutes later with a dog he'd made out of balloons. He then started jiggling this balloon dog up and down between Jack Tinker and I at the bar. By this time, Jack had had enough and took a pin out of his lapel and burst all the balloons. This magician looked at his hand, then looked at Jack and said, 'How childish,' before stomping off. But that's magicians for you, they can be right pains in the arse.

Ian

Magicians really are a bunch of weirdos; you have to be to

spend six hours a day in a room by yourself practising tricks. But amateur magicians are even worse. I was chatting to Jim Bowen when another magician came up to me. He was sporting a huge handlebar moustache and speaking in that clipped manner like an ex-RAF officer, and said, 'Caught the act last night … good start, then you lost them a bit in the middle, managed to get them back, then finished on a high.'

I looked up from my pint and just said, 'Oh, do piss off.' He looked mortified and said, 'That's not very nice. I just thought I'd tell you what I thought.'

Janette

We did meet some great passengers on board though, and our act seemed to go down well. The thing about the QEII is that it isn't all snobby people like the two old dears from Edinburgh who'd been so mortified to see us on board. For many, this is their first time on board and perhaps they've saved up for years for a special anniversary, so the majority of them were great folk and we ended up having a smashing time.

Ian

The cabin was luxury personified too – unfortunately, it spoiled us as, after the QEII, we started working the cruise-ship circuit for Airtours who'd regularly bung us in cabins down in steerage beside the huge turbines. Ah well, there's nothing like coming back to earth with a thump.

Janette

In 2001, we didn't do a panto after a few mix-ups with

different theatres, but we'd never actually spent a Christmas or New Year at home and thought it'd be quite nice for a change. Then a tour operator called asking if we wanted to do the festive season in the Caribbean, and suddenly all notions of a romantic quiet time together in Torquay flew out the window as we thought the Caribbean sounded even better.

So we flew out on 23 December to Miami, but the flight was three hours late in leaving so we missed our connection to Jamaica. The next flight out wasn't for days, so we had to spend Christmas Eve and part of Christmas Day in this hotel in Miami.

Our cruise-ship booker then called and said were to catch another flight on Christmas afternoon.

Ian

I thought the booker said we were going to Puerto Rico, which I thought would be great as we'd been there before and it's a smashing island with fantastic nightlife. However, a real jobsworth of an immigration man wouldn't let us fly because we didn't have a return ticket. Even though I explained we didn't need a return as we were going to catch a boat, he wasn't wearing it and made us buy a return.

Then, on the plane, they announced the flying time, which I thought was pretty long for a little short hop down to Puerto Rico, but thought nothing more of it and we both fell asleep. Just as we were getting ready to arrive, I was looking out of the window thinking, 'This place is looking a bit scabby since the last time we were here,' when the pilot announced it would be ten minutes before we landed in *Costa Rica.*

Once we made it through immigration, all the taxi drivers looked like drug barons. One of them took us to a hotel miles away, which was horrible. So, instead of being on a huge luxury ship in the Caribbean for Christmas night, we were sitting in this cockroach-infested little hotel. In the room which passed for a restaurant, I asked for the menu and the waiter said there was no need for that as there wasn't much food. It was dreadful.

Janette

By this point, I am thoroughly miserable and I've fallen out with Ian – as if it's all his fault – and was wishing that we'd stayed at home for Christmas, instead of starring in a remake of *Planes, Trains and Automobiles*.

Ian

But after a couple of bottles of wine, we'd both mellowed and could almost begin to laugh at the situation. By this point, it's now 2.00am and I said to Janette, 'Come and get a good night's sleep and we'll feel better in the morning.'

But the hotel owner heard this and said, 'No good night sleep – I have to drive you to the boat at 6.00am.'

'Why do we have to leave so early?' I asked.

He simply shrugged and said, 'Because it is seven hours' journey to the boat.'

I thought, 'This trip just gets better and better.'

Sure enough, we left at 6.00am in a beaten-up old bone-shaker of a car, feeling knackered and hungover for the seven-hour journey over countless potholes to the boat. Any spirits we'd manage to raise the night before disappeared on that journey and Janette and I sat practically in silence.

Janette

We travelled right across the whole island that day, through rainforests and over ground that by no stretch of the imagination could be termed a road. It was awful. When we finally got to the boat and prised ourselves off our sweat-soaked seats, the first thing the ship's entertainment manager Lesley said to us was, 'Where have you two been?' We didn't even have to reply as the murderous look on our faces said it all.

But then everywhere we went on the boat, all the punters were saying the same thing to us

'Where have you two been? We were looking forward to your show on Christmas Day.'

Ian

Lesley then told us our cabin was taken as someone else had got in there first. I thumped my case down on the deck and said, 'I'm going to be calm now, Lesley, but if you don't get us our room I'm going to blow.' It was just one of those trips. When the timing has been thrown out of sync, it just has this horrible knock-on effect where everything else turns to crap.

I mean, even the passengers were pains on this journey. Normally on these huge ships, the people are great and we love sitting and chatting to them for hours when we're not working. But what we discovered was that on these Christmas cruises, the ship is full of basically sad, miserable people who don't have friends or family back home; that's why they go away.

So I'm standing on the deck by the rail looking out at the amazing feat of engineering as our huge vessel was being hoisted up 50ft through the Panama Canal, when this bloke from Manchester sidles up beside me, looks at this scene unfolding before our eyes and says, 'Bloody hell, is this all it's about then? I might as well have stayed at home and looked at the Manchester Canal.'

I just shook my head in disbelief. The whole ship was full of moaning, miserable bastards like Mr Manchester Canal. It was dreadful and so unusual from the people we normally met on the ships.

Janette

The best part of it was when we turned up at the San Blas Islands in the West Indies, where the inhabitants, the Kuna Yala Indians, were all my height. I couldn't believe it – a land full of Jimmy Krankies. Not one of the adults could have been over 4ft 7in. The only difference was they had dead skinny legs covered in bangles, while I've got muscular legs from all my dancing. But they were all staring at me in as much amazement as I was staring at them. Then Ian gave me a nudge and said, 'You better keep moving because they're stocktaking.'

Shortly afterwards, we docked in Kingston, Jamaica, then flew to Barbados to meet another cruise liner. But when we got to Customs, a big black female officer asked us to open all our cases when we were in a rush to make our flight. I thought to myself, 'Oh no, not again – I'm not missing another connection.' So I took out my Madonna wig and pointy bra and put them on – the Customs officer just burst out laughing and let us go through.

When we met up with the new cruise in Barbados, we had Hogmanay off so we went out for a meal on the pier with a magician from the ship, Jamie Allan – one of the most normal magicians we've ever met – and his girlfriend Ayesha. It was a beautiful evening and so hot we decided after our meal to go for a swim. When the clock struck midnight, the four of us were all in the water drinking champagne. It was idyllic and finally made the whole trip worth all the hassle.

16

UP FOR THE CRAIC
WITH DAWN

Ian

We weren't sent a script or anything, so we had no idea what French and Saunders were going to do to us. When we turned up at the studio, Dawn French said, 'I'm so pleased you came, I'm so pleased to meet you.' It was the first time ever that someone, who was a much bigger personality than we were, was gushing over us. It took us aback, to tell the truth.

Janette

She said she used to love our shows and used to watch them all. It was a bit like meeting a fan.

Ian

We knew Dawn's husband Lenny Henry, because he had supported us during one of his first ever shows after he won *New Faces* in the early 1970s.

Janette

I asked how Lenny was getting on and she said, 'Oh, he never forgets his time with you playing in Glasgow.' I told her it was funny because I still had a poster with The Krankies top of the bill and Lenny at the very bottom – changed days, eh?

Ian

But I couldn't believe the money that they had spent on this set, it was quality, and we even filmed it in Sheperton studios. Up until then, I hadn't been a big fan of their show, although Janette always loved them. However, I still didn't have a clue what we were doing. I started to get suspicious when I bumped into Roy Hudd, Christopher Biggins and Bernie Clifton – I thought, 'The old acts are all about to get sent up here.'

Janette

It was only then we were told it was a send-up of *Silence of the Lambs*. We didn't think twice, we knew it'd be hilarious. Jennifer Saunders was playing Clarice Starling, the role Jodie Foster played in the film, and Dawn French was, of course, doing Anthony Hopkins' part of Hannibal Lecter.

Jennifer had to walk past all these dingy dungeon cells, with the different variety acts in them. So she walks past Roy Hudd and he sniffs the air and says, 'I can smell …' and instead of saying that disgusting line from the movie that I'm sure you can all remember, he adds '… insecurity. What you need is to get yourself an act and start treading the boards.' Jennifer then gingerly makes her way past Bernie Clifton's cell, who's standing there in his ostrich outfit saying, 'What you need is to get yourself a gimmick – sophistication, that's the name of the game.'

Then she walks slowly past our cell and Ian's sitting on the bed while I'm up at the bars dressed as Wee Jimmy, and say, 'Get yourself a catchphrase ... Fan Dabi Dozi! Fan Dabi Dozi!'

Dawn, as Hannibal, then says to Jennifer, 'What did the Krankies say to you, Clarice?'

She replies, 'Fan Dabi Dozi ... it was horrible.'

Dawn adds, 'I'm sorry about that, Clarice, it won't happen again.'

Janette

I thought their *Silence of the Lambs* sketch and what they got us to do was simply brilliant. Ironically, we were on a plane flying from Perth in Western Australia to Sydney when they showed that episode as part of the in-flight entertainment. All these South Africans were on board and they were howling with laughter, then they realised we were on the flight too, and they all wanted to talk to us.

Ian

Jennifer and Dawn seemed to like the *Silence of the Lambs* sketch so much they invited us back for another movie send-up, this time Batman and Robin alongside Patsy Kensit, who was doing Nicole Kidman's part, while Janette was The Joker and I was Two Face.

Janette

The opening scene was at the gates of the asylum where they wanted my wee hand to come out from between the bars and lift the guard's hat while Ian thumped him with a truncheon, and then Ian was to say 'Fan Dabi Dozi'.

Ian

But during rehearsals, I improvised and said, 'Fan Dabi Dozi – yer bastard.' They loved it and kept it in the sketch, although they bleeped it out – but you still see me mouthing, 'Yer bastard.' Then the prison chief says, 'Oh no – The Krankies have escaped – we need to call for Batman.'

Janette

Then we're supposed to have gatecrashed this posh dinner party, where I've to create mayhem, running around the table making a nuisance of myself, stealing people's jewellery. Every time the camera panned in on me, I had another piece of jewellery dangling somewhere. Ian then says to me, 'Whit's the matter with you?' And I say, 'Uch, I'm just a woman at a bad age.'

Ian

We weren't told what to do, we just ad-libbed it all and they loved it and kept everything in. It was fantastic.

Janette

When I pass by Patsy Kensit, who Jennifer is trying to chat up dressed as Batman, I started pulling childish faces and say, 'Blah, blah, blah.' As soon as the cameras stopped, Jennifer said, 'I'm bringing in my video camera tomorrow to film you doing that – that's just the kind of thing my kids love.' So she did and got me to do that for her video camera.

Ian

They were just lovely people, really down to earth. No angles to them, just straight down the middle. They treated it as a job and wanted to do it as best as they could. They were our sort of people.

Janette

Then they got me back for a third time for a spoof of *Stars Wars. The Phantom Menace*. When Jennifer asked me, I told her straight that I didn't have a clue about *Star Wars* as I'd never seen any of the films. So she sent me a copy of *The Phantom Menace*.

That was in 1999 and we were doing panto at the time in Glasgow, and I went down on my Monday off. When I got there, the studio was roasting because of all the lights. Jennifer was playing Liam Neeson's part of Qui-Gon Jinn, who was to train me up as a Jedi, while I'm Jimmy, creating mischief as usual. The first thing I say is, 'If you're a Jedi, how come you've got such big tits?' I then do the cheeky schoolboy ditty, pointing to all my private parts going, 'Milk, milk, lemonade, round the corner chocolate's made ...'

I also brought down a few props of my own, like a pair of Roy Orbinson glasses that spray water when I sing 'Crying' on stage. I showed Jennifer and she got me to use them too.

As usual with TV sets, there was a lot of waiting about in between takes. We were all in our costumes and it was so hot under the powerful studio lights, especially for Jennifer with all her leather on. It was a big production with a lot of extras but, during the break, Jennifer told me not to go with the other actors on the bus to get some food, instead I was to go back to their own personal trailer. We had a little fan, one of those wee handheld ones, that we passed between the three of us to try and cool down. It came to five at night and we were due to finish at seven, but we were so knackered that the three of us lay down on the bed in their trailer. I'll never forget Jennifer lying on one side dressed as Liam Neeson with the beard, Dawn on the other dressed as Yoda or someone like that (I never did watch that video, so I don't really know who they were playing) and little old me lying in the middle dressed as Jimmy Krankie as usual, passing the fan between each other, and just talking nonsense.

I asked Jennifer if she had a boat in Salcombe and she explained that her and her husband Ade Edmondson have a boat on the Dart but they take it up to Salcombe. I said, 'I knew that because last summer I was in Salcombe and I went into a fruit and veg shop only for the owner to say, "You're the second celebrity we've had in here this week … Jennifer Saunders was in too."' So we promised to look out for each other on the water.

I've got to say, it was one of the most genuine and beautiful moments of my career. They really are fantastic girls and that memory of lying on the bed together will stay with me for ever.

In May 2003, we ended up being invited up to Nobby's Creek again, but this time it was to the set of the ITV show *I'm A Celebrity … Get Me Out Of Here*.

Ian

We were staying in our apartment in Tweed Heads and one day we were in a café by the beach and this Scots guy says, 'I recognise you two.' It turned out he was a producer from the show. We got talking and he thought it'd be a great idea if we came down to the set and Wee Jimmy tried to break in. I thought it sounded fun, but we were in the country on holiday visas at the time and told him this. But he insisted that ITV would take care of it all.

Janette

A few nights later, we then met the show's hosts Ant and Dec in the Tweed Heads Social Club. They're cracking boys but were absolutely knackered as they were working in reverse, staying up all night to do the show live for Britain.

Ian

Every Friday night, Janette and I go to this club for a dance – the type of thing you just can't do at our age back home. But this particular night, we were in with my cousin Robin who was over visiting us, when he spotted Ant and Dec and said, 'Let's go talk to them.' To be honest, I'd only ever seen them a couple of times on the telly and didn't really know what they looked like, especially across a dark, crowded dance floor, so, like a couple of woofters, we waited until we saw Declan Donnelly go into the toilet and followed him in – he must have thought we were at it.

I said to him, 'Excuse me, are you ...' and Dec shouted, 'Wow – it's Ian Krankie ... where's Janette?'

That took me aback a bit, but he was a smashing lad and I told him that she was waiting for someone to dance with, as I've got two left feet. So we went back to the bar and he introduced Ant to us – who's Janette's favourite – and he asked Janette for a dance. She was made up.

Janette

It was brilliant because I was just standing there with Robin's partner Judy, when I got this tap on the shoulder, turned around and it was Ant McPartlin saying in that thick Geordie accent of his, 'Hello, bonnie lass – dae ye fancy a dance?' So we went up for a jig. He was a great laugh.

Ian

Ant and Dec must have been the youngest in the club, but they had a great time. They said they'd heard from their producer that we were in town and asked if we were going to come down and see them on set. I was actually dying to see the place as I'd heard from a few people I knew working on it that it was incredible. A few days later, we got to see it for ourselves and it was something else. There had to be something like 360 people working on it with scores of security staff – a security man even took a picture of our car's registration plate with a digital camera. It was tighter than the Royal protection squads – although that's not saying much these days after that stand-up comedian gatecrashed Prince William's 21st birthday party. In fact, if William wants proper security, he should hire this mob from *I'm A Celebrity*.

But for the sketch, I was to try and lift Jimmy over the fence saying, 'This will get us back on the telly,' before we're rumbled by a security guard, who chases us off – but not before Jimmy gives him a boot in the balls.

Janette

We were only in the jungle for an hour filming and I was eaten alive by bugs. I don't know what they were, but they'd even managed to bite through my socks. I also ended up with a leech on my finger and I'd only just brushed past some bushes. I had literally been mauled just walking from the car park to the set.

On top of all that, it was absolutely freezing and it was pouring down. The producer asked if I'd like to be considered as a participant for a future series, but I'd rather stay in my apartment. It honestly is miserable in the jungle and I wouldn't want to spend any more time in there than I have already.

Ian

We were driving back to Tweed Heads the next day when our journalist friend Matt called on my mobile, saying there had been a story in the Scottish papers along the lines of 'The desperate Krankies try to get back in the limelight by breaking into the set of *I'm A Celebrity*.' As usual, they had quoted an insider saying, 'It was a pathetic attempt to recapture their fame.' I just laughed, as it didn't surprise me. To think we'd make a two-day drive with Janette dressed as Wee Jimmy, to be eaten alive by bugs just to get back on the telly. No thanks. We honestly had no idea how bad the set was until we got there. We had just gone because we'd been invited by some really nice people. But there's no way we'd go through all that just for a TV show – those celebrities are welcome to the jungle.

Ian

Shortly after that, we were asked to take part in a new *I'm A Celebrity Get Me Out Of Here*-style show on ITV called *Drop the Celebrity*. I got a call from some idiot at LWT saying, 'Am

I talking to Ian Krankie? Oh, cool, it *is* you … cool, cool. I'd like you to take part in a new show called *Drop the Celebrity*. What happens is, we take you up in a Hercules …' then speaking to me as if I'm a child, she added, 'Have you ever been up in a Hercules? They're marvellous.'

I deflated her a bit when I said, 'Aye, and bloody freezing. We were up in one with Lenny Henry for Comic Relief.'

She continued, 'Well, there will be people in the audience who vote you off the show, then you'll be kicked out of the plane strapped to an expert in a parachute – it'll be great fun.'

I said, 'Excuse me, let me stop you there. Did you know that we worked for LWT for three years and had our own show on prime-time Saturday night and did three Christmas specials – now you want to throw me out of a bloody plane,' and slammed the phone down. I was furious. Kick us out of a plane indeed – now there's an offer you *can* refuse.

I'm glad I turned them down in such a marked manner. As it turned out, Cheryl Baker from Buck's Fizz agreed to do the show and was the first to be thrown out of the plane and promptly broke her ankle. If that happens to us, then we simply can't work – we'd be stuffed. And I bet the bastards make you sign a waver before you jump. So I'm afraid it may be good for your career to get back on TV, but I ain't sitting around some freezing cold, insect-infested jungle or being thrown out of a plane just to get back on the box – no way.

Janette

I'm sure the public are getting tired of these shows too. It's voyeurism gone mad. They don't have any new ideas. The problem is, they've never nurtured great comedy writers in this country the same way they've done in America with *Friends* and *Frasier* and all the rest. The great talents who can write like Jennifer Saunders stick out like a sore thumb because they are so few and far between. So now we have minor celebrities being booted out of an aeroplane in the name of entertainment. It's sad.

Ian

My young brother Colin is the editor of *TV Times* and he was telling me recently that he was told about a new show where the stars are given enemas, then they hold up a bottle to the cameras so you can see what's been taken out of them. That's the ultimate for me – actually showing shit on TV. Why develop talent when all you literally have to do is show a pile of shit?

17

LET ME ENTERTAIN YOU

Ian

When we got the offer through to appear on *The Entertainers* for the BBC, I must admit I immediately sensed a stitch-up. But my agent assured me that the show would be playing it straight. What I didn't know was that Louis Theroux was one of the producers, or I would have probably said no. But just when you think the tide is turning against the world of political correctness, the BBC is still a bastion of PC. Our contact with the programme was with a director called Harriet and I swear the first words from her mouth were, 'Hi, I'm Harriet and I'm a lesbian – does that bother you?'

'Why would that bother us?' I said. 'We've been in showbiz most of our lives.'

She then explained that she was told she must tell people her sexual orientation before the interviews. I was completely baffled. I then had a question of my own. 'Why do the BBC want to present us as nice people? There must be some edge to this programme.'

'Oh no,' she insisted, 'you've been going for years and it's about time people saw you again.'

Frankly, I wasn't convinced in the slightest.

The first bit of footage they wanted was me taking my 40ft Grandbanks motor cruiser out on the water. I took them on one of the most beautiful boat trips in Britain, from Torquay up the River Dart. But what I noticed was that Harriet and the camera crew weren't interested in any of the scenery whatsoever, and were concentrating on me – they were obviously wanting to catch me off guard. I spotted someone on the water I knew and had a quick chat. Afterwards, Harriet said, 'You seem more at ease with ordinary people than showbiz people – in fact, you're not very showbizzy at all – is Janette more showbizzy?'

When she said that, I knew I should have never agreed to filming.

Then she asked, 'Does it bother you that people don't recognise you any more?'

Again, I was baffled. We've lived in Torquay for years. What was she expecting? The people we see and live with everyday suddenly to ask for our autographs?

Janette

They never used any of that trip on the boat in the show because it was too beautiful. They wanted more of the tacky stuff.

Ian

For the next bit of filming, they wanted to watch us doing a show, so they came down to Great Yarmouth with us, where we were playing the 1,000-seater British Holidays venue at the Seashore holiday camp – it was a fantastic place. Harriet had only been in our car for two minutes with her camera when she said, 'Do you not think it's a big come-down having to play these awful holiday camps?'

I stamped on the brakes and pulled over. I said, 'Now look here, not everyone goes to Tuscany for their holidays like you do at the BBC. This is what ordinary working people do on holiday and, I'll tell you, kids will have more fun here than they would on the Riveria.'

Harriet then asked, 'So will the dads all have tattoos and shaved hair?'

But just before I was going to blow my top, Janette put her hand on mine and said, 'She's just trying to wind you up for the show – don't rise to it.'

So I drove on to the venue without saying another word.

We stopped at a café on the way there and were served by these two big black girls from Birmingham. They were an absolute hoot and were kissing and cuddling Janette saying, 'I can't believe we've met Wee Jimmy Krankie.' And I thought to myself, 'I bet they don't stick that in the show because they want us to be a sad old pair of has-beens that no one recognises,' and sure enough that part never featured either.

We then got there, the organisers had laid on two £35,000 caravans for us and for the BBC and again Harriet just sneered, 'Have they brought out the family silver just to impress us?'

I took her by the arm and said, 'Why are you being like this? All the caravans are like this here. People spend a fortune on them but you would never know that because you'd rather look down your noses at these folk without knowing what they're all about.'

During the rehearsals, she then says, 'Do you know, you've impressed me already – I didn't know you sang.'

I just replied, 'You don't know anything about us – we're more than just a wee boy in a school uniform.'

We then did the show and told the audience the BBC were in filming and, of course, the place went nuts. At the end, there was a queue waiting for our autographs and Harriet said, 'I can't believe it – they loved you.'

That's when I knew for sure they didn't want to show us in good light at all. They thought we'd go on stage and bomb. I said, 'Do you think if we were crap, we would have been around for nearly 40 years? Not a chance.'

Funnily enough, we ended up getting on well with Harriet. She was only doing her job – albeit trying to make us look like fools, but still it was her job. After following us about for weeks, she admitted she wasn't getting the kind of slant she wanted, so she asked if I'd get drunk and she'd film it – well, I don't mind getting drunk on BBC money. So she filmed me getting pissed in our house in Torquay and I played it up for the cameras, jumping into bed and knowing full well that Harriet was a lesbian, I said, 'Come on, Harriet, get yer knickers off and I'll show you a good time.'

Of course, they used that bit! Me acting up like an old lech. But she seemed to be pretty happy with that footage in the end. Of course, I didn't have to give her what she wanted but then she'd have got almost nothing, except a bollocking from her boss, so we helped her out.

Janette

Every time we're interviewed, the journalist or presenter is always after a slant like Harriet. There's not an interview that goes by where they don't ask about our 'curious relationship'. They believe there's something seedy, like all the sleaze that's out now about stars and Internet porn. Well, we had our mad moments, but seedy? I don't think so.

Ian

All we are is an old variety act; there's always been child impersonators in our business, but most people around these days won't remember that. They want to believe there's something dark about us. They can't seem to understand that, at the end of a show, we go home and be ourselves, cook a meal and open a bottle of wine.

Janette

So the only footage they used of me in *The Entertainers* was going shopping in Sainsbury's and getting my legs waxed – gripping television. They focused more on Leo Sayer in the end because he really made a bit of an arse of himself.

Ian

I think they ruined the career Leo had just recently managed to get back. The thing is, I'm more than happy to take the piss out of myself for the likes of French and Saunders, because they're professionals. But this documentary lot are hopeless. Their show looked dreadful and was all done on shaky handheld cameras. It made me feel sick watching it, and the sound quality was dreadful too.

Janette

They didn't like it when we told them what we thought at the screening. They said it was meant to be like that, but I replied, 'I can't believe anyone would deliberately make their show that shaky and practically inaudible.'

When we were making *The Entertainers*, it turned out one of Harriet's friends is the Radio One breakfast presenter Sara Cox. Sara heard Harriet was making this documentary on us and asked me to record a link for some TV show she was doing, with me saying, 'It's Fan-Dabi-Fucking-Dozi.' Now I don't like Sara Cox as she's mentioned us a few times on air and it's always derogatory, calling us the crinkley Krankies or such and such is so ugly he looks like Jimmy from The Krankies. She may think I'm ugly, but at least I'm not a foul-mouthed, chinless wonder like she is. But because Harriet asked me, I said I'd do it, but without the swearing – because I have never sworn on TV in my life. But I couldn't believe it when I then got the short sharp message back from Sara Cox that if I wouldn't swear then she wouldn't use me on her show – as if that was some sort of threat or big deal to me?

I honestly don't mind anyone taking the mick out of me, but people like Sara don't just do that, they're nasty about it. The difference is, Terry Wogan said something like, 'Where are The Krankies now?' On his Radio 2 show – which has millions of more listeners than Sara Cox will ever have or could ever dream of having – and two minutes later he read out an e-mail sent by who knows, saying, 'Actually, The Krankies are top of the bill at The Pavilion Theatre in Glasgow,' and Terry simply added, 'Well, that's great to hear they are still on the go.' Now that's class – something else Sara Cox will never have.

Janette

I was just about to leave Torquay for panto rehearsals at the Glasgow Pavilion for the 2002–03 season when I got this request through from the Channel 4 Japanese betting show *Banzai*. It was fairly straightforward – they wanted Wee Jimmy to show off his boobs!

At first, I thought, 'Nah,' then I discussed it with Ian and decided, 'Well, it's not as if we're childrens' TV stars any more.' Ian also reckoned it would help enhance our 'cult status' if we continued to do more on the university circuit as *Banzai* is a big hit with the students but, to be honest, I never think that way and I did it because I'd always liked the show. I suppose a part of me was also just a little flattered at being offered it in the first place, I mean, Wee Jimmy has had to hide these boobs under a school blazer for nearly 30 years and it was about time they had an airing. Jimmy may not have a willy – but he's got a nice pair of boobs.

But I doubt it raised many eyebrows because it's hardly shocking TV compared to what else is on the telly these days. It was actually really fun to do and completely different from what I'm used to. The producers had asked me to bring an assortment of underwear with me – the first time I've ever been asked to do that before going into a television studio. In the end, they used me in a white bra and, I have to say, the final result was very funny.

A *Banzai* presenter says, in a heavy Japanese accent, 'Today, *Banzai* can reveal a disturbing dark Krankie secret, because he is not really a Wee Jimmy Krankie at all – he actually a woman. But this is good news as it now means we can play A Little Boy Bra Size Bet. For the first time, Wee Jimmy

Krankie man-woman has agreed to reveal his boobs. The question is – what bra size is he? Mr Krankie, man-woman, will you please show us what you've got.'

I then pull apart my blazer, to show off my bra and my only line was to say, 'They're a 34B – Fan Dabi Dozi.'

The *Banzai* presenter adds, 'Wow – look at them, they're unbelievable. Brilliant stuff from the wee fella.'

Ian

At least now everyone can see why I've been hanging around with a cheeky wee schoolboy for all these years!

Janette

We actually got a really good response from that and the *Sun* even did a feature on my strip over two pages. Our friend at the *Sun*, Matt, told me they had had great fun coming up with headlines that day. They originally had 'KRANKIES' KRACKERS' then 'SEE YOURS JIMMY' before finally settling for 'FAN-BOOBY-DOZI.'

It was all good fun and I enjoyed myself with the *Banzai* crew, who really looked after me, getting me first-class rail tickets from Torquay to London and picking me up in a limo. When filming was finished, one chap from the crew escorted me to my limo and, as he closed the door, he immediately got on his mobile, no doubt telling a friend, 'I have just had the weirdest day with Jimmy Krankie.' As the limo pulled away, I lifted up my blouse and gave him another jiggle. He just burst out laughing while everyone else around him looked at him as if he was daft.

But I doubt I'll ever be asked to strip off again, as Wee

Jimmy is getting on a bit, so I reckon he's missed his chance to do *Playboy* – or would that be *Playgirl*?

18

ABSOLUTELY FAN-DABULOUS

Janette

We were in the middle of our Australia break at the start of 2003 when we got a call from the *Ab Fab* office saying that Jennifer Saunders wanted me to play a part in the new series. The good news was that the filming didn't start until we returned, so we didn't have to cut short our trip as I probably would have done because I was so excited about being offered an acting role.

When I got home to Torquay, I called the producer and asked if they had a script yet as it was only two days to filming. The producer Jo Sergeant said, 'Don't be silly – this is Jennifer we're talking about, she changes everything at the last minute,' but Jo promised, if she even had a rough draft, she'd fax it to me before I left on the train to London. When the script came through, there was hardly anything on it, except that I was playing a devil child. The story was that Jennifer's screen daughter Saffy was about to have a baby and Jennifer dreamed the child would be me dressed as the devil.

Then I was told I was also playing a Scottish midwife too. So I learned what few lines I'd been given then, when I arrived in London, I did a readthrough at the studios with Jennifer and Ruby Wax who also works on the scripts for the show. I was unusually nervous as it's actually very daunting walking on to the set of such an established show. I was very nervous and kept saying to Jennifer, 'Please don't give me too many words as I'm only a turn – I'm not an actress.'

But when I came in the next morning for filming, the entire script had been changed again. What's more, Jennifer had done just what I'd pleaded with her not to do, and had given me even more lines. I was going, 'Oh no, Jennifer, what have you done to me?' but she just said I'd be fine and told me to relax.

I had to film the devil baby part first. They had this little lovely blonde three-year-old girl playing one of Jennifer's dream sequences, then a little mixed-race child for one of her other images, as Saffy is supposed to have met up with a black guy, so Jennifer doesn't know what colour the child will be.

The little blonde is wearing an all-in-one romper suit and goes up to Jennifer while she's in bed, then runs away and Jennifer gets up to follow her, but when she catches up with the girl she spins her around and it's me with a blonde wig in a romper suit going, 'Ha, ha … I'm a little baby and I'm coming to get you,' before I pull out a huge knife and Jennifer faints.

Then the doorbell goes and it's me as a midwife and Jennifer gasps, 'It's the devil child,' and I go, 'Oh, scary … scary …' I'm shown to the kitchen and say to them, 'Well, I've got all the blah, blah, blah information that you wanted,' before I spot their fridge full of champagne and add, 'I could murder a drink,' but they only get me a cup of tea.

For my next line, I say, 'Right, I'd better get on with it,' and take a pelvic bone and a baby doll out of my bag and start screaming, 'Ahh … ahhh … more drugs, more drugs,' while squeezing the baby through the pelvic bone. I then tell Saffy, 'I was in labour that long they had to shave me twice. Right, I must be on my way, I've got an antenatal class this afternoon … 30 waddling women squatting on the floor, focusing on their exit holes, all imagining they can breathe their way through childbirth. But I tell them, when push comes to shove, you'll be screaming for drugs and shitting the bed.'

But on my first take, I fluffed that line and just looked at the studio audience and said, 'Oh, fuck it.' The place erupted in laughter. Afterwards, I said to Jennifer, 'I'm really sorry about that,' but, as usual, she was so nice and said, 'Don't worry about it, I always forget my lines and I write them – but Greg Dyke was in the audience and he loved it when you swore.'

I thought to myself, 'That's just perfect, Janette – my grand return to the BBC after all these years and I fluff my lines and swear in front of the Director General.'

But Jennifer was really full of praise. She said the most important thing was that my bottle didn't go and I was able to get the line done on the next take. I suppose that's the thing – I've always had bottle.

There is only one time in my entire career that my bottle went. I did this TV show for Channel 4 with Lulu, which was like a *This Is Your Life*, where they would spring surprises on the star guest, which this week just so happened to be Lulu. They would bring up things from her past, like first loves and relatives. They brought me in because Lulu had won a poetry competition at school and the gag was, 'And here's the child that should have won it,' then I was to walk out to meet Lulu and read her childhood poem.

But for the first time in my life, I choked on my words. I completely froze. It had never happened to me before. But I reckon what had thrown me was that Lulu looked as if she had so much Botox in her face. The shock of suddenly seeing her under the harsh studio lights frightened me rigid and I froze. My bottle had completely gone and I couldn't carry on. Fortunately for me, that show was cancelled and was never screened.

The thing is, Ian and I had met Lulu years before around 1983 when we were in Eilat in Israel. She was in the same hotel with her then husband John Frieda and we'd meet for a drink at night. But I was honestly so shocked at how different she looked now that I couldn't go on. The whole experience upset me for a week. I started to think that maybe I wouldn't be able to go on stage ever again. But, fortunately, it's never happened again – touch wood.

I know a lot of people in showbiz go in for plastic surgery, but I've honestly never considered it. I mean, I could probably do with it, especially since I'm supposed to be playing a wee schoolboy, but really when I do Jimmy now it's a parody of Jimmy Krankie, because by no stretch of the imagination could I honestly pass myself off as a schoolboy now – not with this 55-year-old face. But I'm quite happy with that as now I get new, exciting roles like playing a fearsome old Scottish midwife on *Ab Fab*, so it really doesn't bother me.

I just wouldn't put myself through all that unnecessary pain. I mean, it's injecting poison into your face; who knows what the long-term effects will be? Fortunately, in our line of work, it isn't that common; it's more the acting and singing side of the business that tend to go in for it.

To me, someone like Joanna Lumley gets even better looking with age and she's had nothing done. When I met her on set, I thought she was simply stunning – a real classic-looking woman. And what's more, she couldn't have been nicer to this wee woman from Scotland.

It's great to do these one-off, high-profile TV appearances, but they're just the tip of the iceberg compared with all the other work we do – we basically work all year round, except for our four-month, self-imposed sabbatical in Australia. Summer seasons used to be great fun, renting a little place near Blackpool and doing a couple of shows a day. But all that is dead and buried now. There is no summer season any more. These days, we tour the entire country for the whole summer playing at New Haven caravan sites. The gigs are fine and the bookers put us and our dancers up in fantastic caravans.

However, we'd just started our tour in June 2003 when I thought I'd lost Ian for good. We'd arrived at Butlins in Ayr and I don't know if it's just because we're getting older and slightly more cantankerous, but everywhere we go now there don't seem to be any professional light or sound men. It's just all kids. So when we turned up in Ayr, the lights for the show were all in the wrong position and there was no one around who knew how to set them. Being a former sparky from The Pavilion Theatre, Ian got a set of step-ladders and asked one of the staff members to hold the bottom as he climbed up to adjust the lighting rig. Even though I was watching what he was doing, I still don't know what happened, but the next second Ian seemed to take a little wobble and fell off the top rung of this 15ft ladder.

It was horrible. Everything seemed to be in slow motion as he fell to the ground. He landed awkwardly with a huge thump. I immediately rushed over and told him not to move as I feared he'd broken his neck. He was in shock and was ghostly white, but I made him lie there until an ambulance came. I think I was panicking more than Ian. The worst part was when the medics put an oxygen mask over his face, then put him on a stretcher and carted him into the back of the ambulance. I felt so helpless. You just see everything in your life being reduced to nothing. It's so easy to take each other for granted, but when you think you may lose your partner, the person who's always with you, panic really begins to set in.

We were in Ayr Hospital for hours having Ian checked out and, fortunately, he had just been left with a deep gash in his leg, but I think I was more shaken up than he was. We cancelled the shows for the rest of the week, but Ian insisted he got back on stage after just five days' rest – with stitches in his 8in wound.

So now I've banned him from going up any more ladders in the future. I don't care if the lights are in the wrong position – we'll perform in the dark if we have to.

Our shows still go down well. We do a very fast one-hour set. The longest thing in the act is Wee Jimmy, which lasts for about 20 minutes. Jimmy still gets the biggest reaction. Parents bring their kids in and say, 'This is what your mummy and daddy used to watch.' If we didn't do Jimmy, there would be a riot.

Ian

We've always done well with working-class people, they are our audience. We are working-class entertainers and we've never been high-brow. We come on with our dancers and perform hits from the charts and then we finish up with Austin Powers with me as Dr Evil and Janette as, who else, but Mini Me.

People probably look down their noses at acts like us playing holiday camps, but there's nothing else left now in this country. There is no summer season now. People who used to do the piers are now working the ferries or the holiday camps like us.

Janette

The camps are a good money-maker for us, but it's hard work. It's like having a proper job – every day we get up and have to hit the road, set up the gear, work 'til midnight then do it all over again. A friend of mine, who works in a bank, said, 'But, Janette, that's what most people have to do. They are routined – you've just been very privileged that you've only had to work for a couple hours a day most of your life.'

Ian

But being on tour we're always playing pranks on each other. I remember one time taking our keyboard player, Ian Cundell, on a tour of Australia in 1998. He was knocking about with one of the dancers at the time and ended up getting a dose of thrush. Being young and none the wiser, he asked me what he should do and I said he needed to get a bottle of Dettol and a toothbrush and scrub it off. He looked petrified but went to a store and bought the Dettol and a toothbrush and came back to the hotel to scrub his privates. I was just about to let him go through with the prank when I thought better of it in case he did his willy some serious damage – his girlfriend would have never talked to me again.

Anyway, three years later, when we were playing Ayr's Gaiety Theatre, Ian Cundell told our writer Russell Lane about the prank I'd played on him. So they came up with a plan to get me back and wrote me a letter from a besotted fan called Diana. The letter was drenched in perfume and was begging me to spend the night with her when she came up to see the show. I showed Janette the letter and she reckoned it was just some nutcase and told me just to ignore it. But then I received another one from Diana saying that she had just finished with her husband and was now determined to have me when she came to see me that very night.

I was starting to get worried and when I walked through the front of the theatre Russell was standing there with this beautiful girl, whom he introduced as Diana. I didn't know what to do, as I didn't know if she was a loony or whatever, so I showed her around the theatre. All the time she's deeply unnerving me as she just keeps staring at me.

Then, that night, when we're on stage, Diana's sitting by herself blowing me kisses all through the act. I come off stage and start getting a really hard time from Janette. She's shouting at me, 'What have you got going on with this girl? Have you slept with her?' Of course, unbeknown to me, Janette was also in on the gag.

Afterwards, we all go to a pub called Christina's and meet up with all these actors from The Civic Theatre. I'm telling them all about this psycho Diana when suddenly she turns up, sits beside me and starts rubbing my leg. Janette's drawing me daggers, so I nip up to get a round in and I tell the bar staff the problem. They just shrugged and said, 'Well, having a stalker is just the price of fame, Ian' – those bastards were in on the joke too.

Eventually, they couldn't keep it going any longer and the whole place fell about laughing. Of course, I couldn't leave it there and the next day I got my cousin Robin, who has quite a distinguished voice, to phone up Ian Cundell and pretend to be a policeman investigating reports of a stalker. When Ian revealed to the 'policeman' that it had all been just one big joke he was threatened with being charged with wasting police time. He was getting really flustered until Russell Lane grabbed the phone and called the inspector's bluff.

Afterwards, I asked Russell how far he would have been prepared to take the wind-up. It turned out that, had he got away with it, the next stage was to have this actress friend of his turn up at Turnberry where we were all going to play golf, and pull a fake gun on me and shout, 'You promised you'd leave Janette,' before shooting me with the starter pistol. I'd have probably died from a heart attack. You've got to watch these buggers for their wind-ups on tour. They'll wait years to get their own back on you.

Janette

After popping up on various TV shows in 2002 and 2003, we got all these offers to play big bars like Brannigan's in Manchester. Jade from *Big Brother* had been at this venue the week before and was supposed to do half an hour but only lasted 12 minutes.

The week before that, they had Spencer from *Big Brother* and paid him £2,000 just to stand and chat to people at the bar. But they wanted us to do our act.

Well, the place was packed to the rafters and the DJ forgot to put our mini-disc on, so instead he just shouted, 'Give it up for the Krankies.' Just at that moment, there was a fight in the corner and the place was quickly turning into a riot. We surrendered after 40 minutes and couldn't wait to get out. It was just horrendous. The lights and sound were terrible and the crowd weren't interested – they were also all standing up so no one could see me. So we quietly left by the back door.

Ian

The next day, the bar owners, Hendersons, phoned up asking us to do all the Brannigan's bars across the country for £2,000 a gig. We couldn't believe it because it had been crap. They didn't mind as the venue had been packed out – that's all they cared about. But we turned them down flat. We're too old to be doing all that nonsense now.

Janette

In the same year, we were asked to do our first university gig at Strathclyde Uni. There was a stand-up act who had been a big hit at the Edinburgh Festival who was supposed to do half an hour before us – and he lasted just six minutes. All he did was eff and blind and the students simply didn't want that.

I have never been so nervous before a job in all my life. I was terrified, especially after this comic died on his arse. But that all disappeared as soon as we went on stage and there was this almighty cheer from everyone shouting, 'Fan Dabi Dozi.' I then walked through the audience and, instead of looking for 'me mam', I was looking for my sister. Ian asks, 'What's she like?' and I say, 'Bacardi Breezers …' – the students loved it.

This huge guy stood up in front of me and I said, 'Hello, big boy – do you know I'm the only person who could ever go up on you.' Well, that was it, the place just erupted. It just shows, you don't have to swear. In fact, we only swore once that night and that was only for the students. It was while we were doing the magic act and Ian tells me to get into the box and he'll pass a sword through my head and I shout 'Get tae fuck.' But that was it.

Ian

What was interesting was that all the audience were boys – there were only three girls in the crowd and we'd never realised until that moment that Jimmy Krankie must have been a boys' act. You can never tell when you do panto because the whole family is there and we only do Jimmy for a little while, if at all.

I suppose it was like Dennis the Menace – Jimmy was a boy's hero.

EPILOGUE

Janette

Well, this has pretty much been our whole life story so far. It's funny though, because I've met people who think Ian and I haven't had a life at all, because we never started a family and lived like nomads, constantly moving about, moving houses, living out of suitcases. Someone once said that we had a 'funny way of life'. But it has been funny, because we have had laugh upon laughs.

Ian

I don't remember a day that's gone past where we haven't laughed. How many couples can say that? Even when Janette's mum was ill, we'd still break the tension at some point of the day by having a chuckle, because that's just the way we are.

Janette

Of course, we've had fights, really big barneys, but we've only fallen out for a day at the most. Ian and I never hold grudges, especially against each other. We talk about things if there's something annoying us, which people from our generation tend not to do. They'd rather just go in a huff and not speak, but what does that solve?

Ian

If we're angry, we'll have a right good swear at each other – call each other all the bastards of the world. You'd be surprised how calm you feel after having a right little swear-fest.

Janette

But after that, we'll then listen to each other – and I mean listen, not shouting over the top of what we're trying to say, and then talk about it. But what I can't believe is that, since meeting Ian when I was 19, all those years have passed so quickly.

Ian

That's really why we want to stop, or at least slow down with the work. We want to appreciate more of our time together.

Janette

Don't get me wrong, I love our work, really love it, but I don't want to do work that I don't want to do, if that makes any sense. Because we've done some great jobs and I don't want to take jobs just for the sake of them. We think we've been quite sensible with our lives and have had a pension fund for years. We got nice property and everything's paid for; we don't want to be one of those acts that just goes on and on and on. We work now to keep our lifestyle. I don't think we could keep the same lifestyle – which, basically, means we can go and do what we want – if we retired, but we'd still be comfortable.

Ian

I would say we've had a lucky life. To be able to do what we have, we're the luckiest people in the world. What I hate in this business is the people who moan, like some of these young *Pop Idol* or *Pop Star* reality-TV acts, they actually moan if one of their records doesn't get to number one. We were just delighted to have a hit record in the first place. Who cares if it didn't go to number one?

In 1978, Janette and I were in a swimming pool in Jersey at three in the morning with four of our dancers all drinking champagne, having a barbecue overlooking a beautiful bay. And we weren't even famous at that point. I remember saying to Janette, 'This really is the life – I wonder what'll be like if we ever get famous and successful?' The thing is, it never got any better, it was always that good.

Janette

That's why we loved Jersey so much. We really lived the high-life – not a pretentious, social-climbing high-life, we were never into that. I just mean we mixed with some fantastic people and did some fantastic things that we simply wouldn't have done if I'd stuck to my office job back in Glasgow all those years before.

Ian

To be honest, when we did become famous, it was really just a hindrance as it restricts the fun you can have – in case we got caught. Nowadays, it appears that people just want the fame and the money. They don't want even to work for the fame, they just want to turn up for a few auditions then end up on a Saturday night TV show then go to number one, all in the space of a few weeks. We had to serve an apprenticeship, if you like, working for years and years around the clubs, making our mistakes and learning from them, not making our mistakes in front of millions of TV viewers.

Janette

The thing is, half of these *Pop Stars* or *Pop Idol* acts are not particularly talented. A handful have beautiful voices, but it takes more than that. You need charisma and personality – all these things go into making the truly great performers. I'm not for a moment saying we're in that category, but I know what works on stage, what gets laughs and how to control a theatre full of children screaming from the rafters.

Ian

These TV shows tell 17-year-old kids that they're big stars. I've actually heard them say, 'You are a star,' when they're not; they're only standing on the first rung of their career ladder. What people are falling for now is the fame. We honestly never looked for the fame and I mean that.

As I said, what could be better than having a 3.00am champagne barbecue with four lovely dancers – who needs the fame? All we ever wanted to do was to be the best at whatever level we were performing at. We got great fun out of creating shows.

Our manager, Stan Dallas, once said to us that if someone has been in the business for 35 years, then they have to be good as there's no way they can con the public and the promoters for that length of time. If they were crap, they would have been out of the business 30 years ago. Well, we now fall into that veteran performer category and I'd like to think that the people who come to see us leave thinking the same. That we were actually pretty good. That we made them laugh. I still love it when people come up to us, surprised, and say, 'You were great tonight!' We're always grateful for their comments and even their reaction as we know they'll go and tell their friends and that keeps us in work.

But what's more pleasing to us when we do a panto now is when the kids, who've never seen us on the telly, come up and know our names, just because they saw us the year before in panto.

Janette

When I go on stage now, all the kids know I'm a woman, but they forget straight away when I'm playing Buttons or Wishy Washy and I love how kids get right into pantos that way.

Ian

Our lives are so much more fun now because we don't have the pressure to be successful hanging over us, as we always had with television. In a way, it's like the good days at the start of our career.

Janette

I've seen people who started out at the same time and are still at the top, but they are consumed with fear. 'What if I don't have my show commissioned next year?' and it eats them up. Well, I've been through all that and I never want to go through that again. Even the occasional year when we're not asked back to do panto, then that's fine with us. We just think, 'Well, we'll have Christmas off.' We don't worry about it any more. People on TV might make a lot more money than us, but who cares? We're comfortable, and how much money do you really need?

Ian

Les Dennis went down a different route from us and had a lot of big breaks – through luck more than anything else, because it wasn't through talent and I am not trying to be nasty about the guy. But, to me, he was always a lightweight compared to his comedy partner Dustin Gee. He was the straight man. He's was on television for all these years and even did that awful *Celebrity Big Brother* in 2002. But Les now has no life. He left his first wife for a young actress, Amanda Holden, who has left him and he's off the TV now and a figure of ridicule. We don't mind being ridiculed because, as I've said, at least people remember us to slag us off in the first place. But Les should have been doing what we are doing now and taking it easy instead of still desperately trying to punt himself for TV. That's a mistake because most people only get one shot on the telly, then it chews them up and spits them out. The trick is to establish yourself in the time you have on television and make the most of it – not to keep wanting more.

258

EPILOGUE

Janette

That's the thing that kills me about showbiz marriages. Les and Amanda were married seven years and it was hailed as a lifetime in showbiz circles. God knows what that makes ours.

Ian

As for the future? I think we'd like to do after-dinner speaking as we get older when it'll become harder for us to run around on stage like crazy.

Although we have found lately that we're getting more and more offers to do the university circuit. They're incredible gigs and it's great to hear all these students sing along to 'Fan Dabi Dozi'.

Our so-called cult status has probably been enhanced by doing shows like Jonathan Ross's *It's Only TV But We Like It* – Jonathan was very funny and a great talent – and *The Frank Skinner Show*, where Frank dressed up as me with a curly wig and the comedian Rhona Cameron dressed as Jimmy Krankie and we all performed 'Fan Dabi Dozi' together.

That was after Tony Blackburn had said Rhona looked like Jimmy on the ITV series *I'm A Celebrity ... Get Me Out Of Here*.

Frank Skinner also interviewed us beforehand, although that part was never shown as they wanted to give more time to their other guest Geri Halliwell. I'm glad they ditched our interview as I didn't think he was very good. He's got very cold eyes and was always looking straight through us. You could almost see the cogs of his brain moving as he tried to think of his next line. It doesn't make for a brilliant interview technique and I must say I didn't rate Skinner much as a chat-show host.

Janette

But I don't care what people think and I don't care too much for chat shows either – as it's always the same old questions. I also never worry about things like, 'Where will I be in ten years time?' I never have thought like that. I mean, I know what I'll be doing next Christmas, as we've been asked back to do panto, but we've never had a game plan. After panto, we go out to Australia where we do 11.00am shows for pensioners and finish by 1.00pm to hit the golf courses. And if we decide not to do that, as we did in 2003, then we just have four months off instead and greatly improve our golf handicap. It's perfect.

Ian

My only real regret in this business was back in 1990 when the director of *KTV* at Borders telly asked me to do a cookery programme to be networked on ITV, as he used to love the meals I'd make for him after filming, but I wasn't that keen. So he then went and sourced this old farmhouse with a cracking traditional kitchen for me to use. He also had an idea of using Janette in the show as she'd do the shopping for me and then celebrities would come over for dinner. They were desperate for me to do it but, as I've said, telly was never the be-all and end-all for me and, at the time, I was knackered as I'd just done a panto. So I turned them down. The next thing, all these cookery programmes sprung up on every channel. But that's life; it obviously wasn't meant to be, although cooking remains one of my favourite passtimes.

I started cooking the first time I met Janette after realising that she couldn't cook to save herself. She had taken me to her home in Queenzieburn and made me soup, which was so thick the spoon could stand up in it. Ever since then, the kitchen was always my domain. My friend Joan, who was a chef, also taught me a lot. But if you love something, then you pick it up really easily.

Janette

Ian's got a real flair for cooking. He's amazing. He's the type who can taste any dish in a restaurant and know every ingredient that was used in it. He also knows how to improve them too. He's a total perfectionist. He was making a curry for 12 people in Australia once and didn't like the taste so he slung the whole lot out just two hours before our guests arrived – John Inman was one of them – then ran about daft getting another one made just in time. He was determined that no one was going to leave our apartment saying the food was rubbish.

He also made a lovely red snapper dish for Max and Blossom Bygraves, which they still go on about. So I'd love to see Ian have his own cookery show, especially if he could make it in Australia as the produce is so fantastic down there. He cooks almost every night rather than go out. He just loves cooking.

Ian

We love our time in Australia. We get up at 7.00am every morning and go for a walk, come back and have a bowl of fresh fruit and cereal, do the shopping for the dinner that night, nip off to the beach for a couple of hours' swimming, come back for a light lunch then go and play golf at about three in the afternoon when it's slightly cooler. Then it's a couple of beers in the clubhouse and home for half-seven to watch the telly and cook – that's the life.

Janette

But we're determined now that when we go down to Australia we're not working there any more. I think that at our age we should be able to take four months a year off. It does us the world of good. We go out on the golf course and talk about new things to do with the act. We also have time to visit the big casino shows and pick up new ideas. When you're working, you never get a chance to see any other shows.

Ideally, I would eventually like to spend nine months a year down there and three months working back home.

Ian

I would love to see Janette doing more acting like *Absolutely Fabulous*, because she's a tremendous talent. I think she'd be perfect as an abusive bag lady for *Last of the Summer Wine* – although most wives would kill their husbands for saying so.

But, in the end, no matter what we do or where we end up, we will always be The Krankies and that's fine by us, because we've had a laugh along the way and hope we've created a few too.

In fact, if I was being really corny, you could say our strange way of life has been absolutely Fan Dabi Dozi!